Elizabeth Hayward & Liam Peterson

THE VEGAN FITNESS COOKBOOK

135 new plant-based recipes for muscle growth, super workouts, high protein energy and fat burning. The healthy way to be vegan athletes with golden tips for men and women

Table of Contents

INTRODUCTION

Congratulations on purchasing *The Vegan Fitness Cookbook* and thank you for doing so.

The following chapters will discuss how easy it is to consume a vegan diet and be a top athlete at the same time. You can be a vegan and be an athlete too. The key to doing this is having the knowledge of which foods to eat and in what combinations to eat them, so that you will be able to be a top performer in whatever athletic endeavor you chose to participate in. This book will give you that knowledge and show you how easy and how delicious a vegan diet can really be.

One of the greatest concerns for athletes considering a vegan diet is the protein intake that is needed to fuel top performance and healthy muscle tone, especially for weightlifters and bodybuilders. But this book will show how the vegan diet will offer enough of all of the necessary nutrients to make it a valid consideration for any athlete.

There are plenty of books on this subject on the market, thanks again for choosing this one! Every effort was made to ensure it is full of as much useful information as possible, please enjoy!

CHAPTER 1: THE VEGAN LIFESTYLE FOR ATHLETES

WHY CHOOSE A VEGAN DIET?

Veganism, the practice of following a vegan diet and/or lifestyle, means avoiding animals and animal products. Those who eat a vegan diet will not eat any kind of animal products or any products that are made from animal products. Those who follow a vegan lifestyle will not only eat a vegan diet, but they will also refrain from wearing clothing made from animals or using any products that either come from animal products or are tested on animals.

Those who adopt the vegan diet will not eat any red meat, poultry, pork, fish, seafood, fowl, dairy, eggs, or any other product that comes from animals or animal products. This also means no more honey, gelatin salad, or sugar. Many products may be vegan in nature, like sugar that comes from a plant, but the process used to make it ready for human consumption involves using animal products.

Athletes have special nutritional needs that must be met if they are to perform at a high level. One of the considerations of athletes following a vegan diet is that the intense level of athletic activity might lead the athlete to suffer from an immune system that has been mildly suppressed. This can lead athletes to be more susceptible to acquiring viral and bacterial infections that might compromise their training. Since plant foods are naturally higher in properties that will boost the immune system than animal products are, the vegan athlete will likely enjoy many fewer sick days than his meat-eating opponent.

Athletes are also at an increased risk of oxidative stress, which is an imbalance between the antioxidants and the free radicals in the body. Free radicals are molecules that are formed during the normal process of metabolism inside the body. During the metabolic process, some cells are damaged but not killed, and these cells are called free radicals. They float around in the human body and look for places to cause damage. Free radicals are responsible for everything, from inflammation to cardiovascular disease. Antioxidants are compounds that inhibit the chemical reaction of oxidation that produces free radicals that can damage the body. Plant-based foods are loaded with antioxidants. A well-planned vegan diet can be beneficial to athletes in terms of helping them recover better and faster after an exercise session or an athletic event.

THE BENEFITS OF THE VEGAN DIET

People who follow the vegan diet have a significantly less risk of developing some sort of cardiovascular disease. Many of the health problems that are related to cardiovascular disease begin with poor diet and obesity. While obesity may not necessarily be a problem for most athletes, eating a diet that is high in red meat and saturated fat is a poor diet that can lead to health problems, no matter how strong or proficient an athlete is. Seemingly healthy athletes who have amazing stamina and fantastic body structure have developed some sort of cardiovascular disease, usually something that affects the heart. A poor diet can lead to high blood pressure, high cholesterol, and the buildup of plaque, all of which can contribute to cardiovascular disease.

The vegan diet, with its emphasis on Plant-based foods, will give you all of the carbs, fats, and proteins that your body needs to perform along with all of the minerals, vitamins, and antioxidants your body needs, without all of the added unhealthy fats and sugars. The key is to base your daily diet on whole foods instead of processed vegan substitutions. A veggie burger or vegan cheese is fine once in a while, but they should never be a regular part of your diet. It is possible to gain weight on a vegan diet by eating too many off the foods that are not good for you. You will only reap the full benefits of the vegan diet if you stick to whole, Plant-based foods and try to stay away from any processed foods. The available choices on the vegan diet are numerous, and you are only limited by your own taste buds and imagination.

TOP FOODS FOR MUSCLE GROWTH

There are plenty of vegan foods that will help you to build the lean muscles that you want. You will want to get a variety of good Plant-based foods in your diet while making sure that you are eating enough of the protein-rich plant foods that will help you build and maintain muscle strength. You will not only want to consume foods that are high in protein, but you will also need to eat extra amounts of food so that you have a surplus to help you gain muscle growth. The vegan diet for bodybuilding is higher in its protein content than the regular vegan diet. And the protein that comes from plants is not as high in its quality as the protein that comes from animals. But with the right planning, you will be able to consume the right amounts of foods and proteins to help you reach your goal.

When you are planning your meals with the goal of building muscle, you will need to make sure that your intake of protein and fats are sufficient to aid in muscle growth. Proteins are made from amino acids, and these are compounds that your body needs in order to build muscle. Unfortunately, vegan protein sources normally do not contain all of the essential amino acids that the body will need. You will also want to maintain a regular intake of fat because your body needs fat in order to be able to absorb the nutrients from the protein. And the fat in your foods will help to add needed calories for the bodybuilder. You will also need to ensure that you are drinking plenty of water because Plant-based foods are high in fiber, and you will need the extra water to help move the fiber through your body.

There are foods that will specifically provide you with the right amounts of protein that you need in order to maintain and build your muscles.

Beans and Chickpeas – Beans, which include pinto beans, black beans, kidney beans, and navy beans, and chickpeas, also known as garbanzo beans, contain high amounts of protein in every serving. One cup of any bean will give you two hundred twenty-seven calories and fifteen grams of protein. They are good sources of fiber and complex carbs. Chickpeas and beans provide you with high amounts of phosphorus, which helps your body carry needed nutrients to the cells, and potassium, which your body needs for the proper contraction and function of your muscles.

Edamame, Tofu, and Tempeh – These products are all made from soybeans, which are a good source of protein. Edamame is the soybeans in their immature state, and they have a slightly grassy and sweet taste. Edamame will need to be boiled or steamed before they are eaten. They can be added to salads or soups or eaten on their own. Tofu easily absorbs the flavors of the foods that it is paired with, which is a good thing because tofu does not have much flavor of its own. It is made from cooking and fermenting bean curds and then pressing them together into a patty or a square shape. Tempeh is made in the same way and has a slightly nutty flavor. Tempeh and tofu can be added to many different recipes like chili, burgers, and soups. Tofu can be used as a substitute for eggs to make a scrambled breakfast dish. Since all of these items come from soybeans, their nutritional value is the same. Three and one-half ounces of edamame contain one hundred twenty calories and eleven grams of protein. Tofu has one hundred seventy-seven calories in three and one-half ounces with fifteen grams of protein. And tempeh has fifteen grams of protein and one hundred sixty-two calories. They are all good sources of iron, which helps your body to make collagen, which is the main component in your connective tissues.

Green peas – Just one cup of this side dish contains nine grams of protein and just one hundred twenty-five calories. And peas will provide just over twenty-five percent of your daily requirement of fiber. Peas do not cause the spikes in blood sugar than many other starches cause because they are also full of fiber. Peas are good in salads, soups, stews, stir-fries, casseroles, and as a side dish.

Hempseed – While hemp seed comes from the same family of plants as the marijuana plant, it carries only slight trace amounts of THC. One ounce will provide you with ten grams of protein that are easy to digest and considered to be complete. A complete protein contains all nine of the essential amino acids, the ones that your body does not make itself that must come from food. Hempseeds are also a good source of magnesium, which has many benefits to offer the human body. Magnesium helps to build strong bones and teeth. It works alongside calcium to regulate the contraction of your muscles. And it assists with the clotting of your blood. And hemp seeds are a good source of omega-3 and omega-6 fatty acids that will help to reduce inflammation in your body. Sprinkle hemp seeds on your cereal or blend them into your smoothies.

Lentils – One cup of cooked lentils has eighteen grams of protein and two hundred thirty calories. Lentils can be used in almost any type of dish. They can be used as an ingredient in soups, stews, and stir-fries. Cold cooked lentils are a great addition to salads. Cooke lentils can be mashed with avocado or chickpeas to make a dip or a spread. And that same one cup of lentils has about fifty percent of the daily fiber intake recommended for adults. Lentils are a good source of vitamin B9, also known as folic acid or folate, which your body needs in order to grow new cells.

Nutritional Yeast – This is a deactivated strain of yeast, so it won't grow inside your body, and you can buy it in flake form or powder form. It has a nutty, cheesy flavor, so it is often used in vegan dishes that require some form of cheese or garnish like tofu scrambles and salads. One ounce of nutritional yeast provides your body with seven grams of fiber and fourteen grams of protein. Nutritional yeast reduces inflammation and supports your immune system.

Quinoa and amaranth – Although these are often referred to as ancient grains because their chemical makeup has not changed much over the years, they are not grown from grasses like the other cereal grains do. One cooked cup of either one provides about two hundred twenty-five calories and nine grams of protein. Both are also sources of complete proteins, which is a rare find in the grains group. And both are also good sources of fiber and complex carbs.

Seitan – This is a popular source of protein for vegans that is made out of wheat gluten. Unlike many of the fake meats that are made out of soy, seitan has the texture and appearance of meat when it is cooked. Seitan is also known as wheat gluten or wheat meat. Three and one-half ounces of seitan contains twenty-five grams of protein and only three hundred seventy calories. That protein level makes seitan one of the richest sources of plant protein available to vegans. Seitan is an excellent source of selenium, which is a necessary mineral that neutralizes free radicals in your body. This mineral will also work with your thyroid gland to keep your metabolism functioning well. Seitan is easily found in most health food stores or specialty grocery stores in their refrigerated section. If you would prefer to make your own seitan, you can use vital wheat gluten to make it. Seitan is a great meat substitute, not only for the protein content, but also for its appearance when cooked, because seitan can be grilled, sautéed in stir-fries, or pan-fried. It should not be eaten by anyone with celiac disease or gluten insensitivity.

Spirulina – This is an alga that is full of nutrients. Two tablespoons of spirulina will give you eight grams of complete protein along with many other nutrients that your body needs. And spirulina will help to stabilize your blood pressure, reduce inflammation, and strengthen your immune system.

Teff and Spelt – These are two of the grains that are known as ancient grains, which are a small group of grains that have not been changed much by selective breeding. Teff comes from an annual grass, which means that it is free of gluten, but spelt contains gluten because it is a form of wheat. One cup of spelt will provide you with two hundred forty-six calories and eleven grams of protein, while teff provides a whopping seven hundred eight calories and twenty-five grams of protein. Teff and spelt are used as alternatives to more common grains and can be used in recipes ranging from risotto to polenta to baked goods.

TOP FOODS FOR ENERGY

Any type of athlete, no matter what athletic pursuit they follow or how rigorous their training schedule is, will need to maintain good levels of energy in order to get through their workouts. Fortunately, there are plenty of vegan foods that will provide high energy to athletes while still maintaining the vegan diet requirements. Whether you need energy for your daily needs or to get through a strenuous workout, try adding some of these vegan foods to your diet.

Almonds – These nuts are full of nutrients that will help boost your energy levels like manganese, which helps your body to metabolize the food that you eat. They are also good sources of fiber, magnesium, riboflavin, copper, and protein. Almonds are full of fiber and healthy fats, which will keep you feeling fuller for longer, and they will help to regulate your blood sugar. Almonds are a great snack food, but they are also very useful in recipes. Slice almonds to use with chia pudding or oatmeal. They are also delicious in pasta or salads.

Cacao – Cacao is like cocoa because both come from the cacao bean, but cacao is not another name for cocoa or another type of cocoa. Cacao is the powder that is made by crushing the raw cacao beans, where cocoa comes from crushed roasted cacao beans, and the process of roasting destroys many of the benefits that you might get from cacao. It will give you the flavor of chocolate without giving you all of the chemicals or sugar. The chocolate flavor will activate the hormones in your brain that cause you to feel good and happy. And cacao has a high content of iron that will help your body to bring oxygen to your organs and muscles, and that will help you to feel energetic and alert. Cacao is a marvelous ingredient in smoothies or your morning oatmeal.

Chia Seeds – While all seeds will give you a great boost of energy, chia seeds will provide you with healthy omega-3 fats, protein, and fiber. The lack of carbs will help to keep your blood sugar levels constant while helping to boost your energy levels. Chia seeds have almost no taste, and they can be added to almost anything. Mix chia seeds with the non-dairy milk of your choice and some fruit to make a delicious pudding. Put chia seeds into a salad, a smoothie, or vegan yogurt. Chia seeds also go well with other foods that will boost your energy like cacao, nut butters, and fruit.

Fresh Fruit – The fiber content of fresh fruit combined with simple sugars makes fresh fruit nature's ultimate energy bar. The sugar and fiber combined in the fruit will allow your body to release energy slowly over a longer period of time, which will help you to feel full and energetic for much longer. Try to eat a wide variety of fruit because each individual fruit will provide its own unique mix of minerals and vitamins. Apples digest slowly to help you feel full of energy longer. Oranges are a good source of vitamin C, and bananas will provide you with fiber and potassium. Fruit makes a great snack that you can take anywhere, or you can make it part of a meal by mixing it into a smoothie or tossing it into your salad.

Lentils – This high energy food is full of both fiber and protein. They have a low amount of carbs, which will help to stabilize your blood sugar and help to prevent crashes and spikes of energy. Lentils are a great Plant-based source of protein since twenty-six percent of the calories come from protein. They cook quickly and are a good ingredient for high energy vegan meals. Use lentils instead of ground beef when you make a sauce for your spaghetti. Lentils are also great for making soup.

Nut Butter – These come in a variety of options like almond butter, cashew butter, sunflower butter, and peanut butter. They are all high in protein and in the good fats and fiber that will keep you feeling full for longer and provide you with energy. Make sure to read the ingredients on the nutrition labels because some nut butters are full of added sugars in various forms. Look for ones that are made with all-natural ingredients.

Oats – Oats are a favorite of people who work out because they are filling, easy to make, and very inexpensive. Oats will provide you with magnesium, which helps with your muscle contractions. They also contain potassium, iron, and several of the B vitamins. The best choices are rolled oats or steel-cut oats, which soak up liquid better and have a lower glycemic index than instant oats, so even though they take longer to cook, they are great for a high energy snack or meal. If you would like something more than a simple bowl of oatmeal, to make cookies or granola bars with the oats and add dried bits of fruit. Dress up your bowl of oatmeal with cinnamon or fruits, and don't overlook overnight oats.

Spinach – This veggie carries five grams of spinach in every cup. Spinach is also full of calcium, magnesium, potassium, folate, iron, and vitamin A. These nutrients will provide needed energy for those intense workouts and long days. Spinach will keep you full, stabilize your levels of blood sugar in your blood, and help you to build muscles. Spinach is a great addition to smoothies if you want the benefits but aren't wild about the taste. If you like the taste of spinach, you can put it into a salad, steam it for a side dish, or chop it finely and cook it into eggs or pasta.

Sweet Potatoes – This is another high-energy staple food that bodybuilders like to eat. The amount of carbs balances perfectly with the fiber, vitamin C, and vitamin A. The carbs in sweet potatoes will keep your blood sugar level for hours and help you to avoid spikes and crashes. You can make them into fries, bake them, or put them into curries.

TOP FOODS FOR FAT BURNING

People who follow a vegan diet have a decided advantage over meat-eaters when it comes to weight loss because the staples of the vegan diet are full of fiber, while foods that come from animals have no fiber. While adding very little or even no calories, fiber will control your appetite and keep your digestive tract clean and healthy. A diet that is high in fiber will help you to lose weight while it helps diminish the risk that you will develop diabetes, high blood pressure, or heart disease. Plant food diets are high in fiber, water, and complex carbs, which will make you feel full for longer periods of time and will also help your body to create energy even when you are resting. There are some foods that are the best at what they do when it comes to helping you burn fat and lose weight.

Almonds – All nuts will help to suppress your appetite, but almonds are the best for maximizing digestive flow and burning fat. Eating just twenty almonds each day will help to decrease your appetite since they are low in carbs. And almonds are high in fiber, which means that they will pass through the body quickly and help to keep your digestive tract clean.

Avocado – Many times, when people are trying to lose weight, they will avoid eating avocados because the fruit does contain twenty-one grams of fat. However, the avocado is the only fruit that contains monounsaturated fat, which is the good fat that will help to lower your cholesterol. The avocado is also eighty percent dietary fiber. Eating just half an avocado will make you feel less hungry longer and will make you less likely to overeat. And the monounsaturated fats in avocadoes will help to prevent fat from collecting around your abdomen.

Black Beans – All beans contain fiber while being low in calories, but black beans are some of the best for burning fat in your body. The compounds in food that play a significant role in managing your weight by interfering with the absorption of glucose in your body are higher in black beans. They are also a good source of vegan protein while providing you with six grams of fiber in one cup that has just one hundred calories. And the resistant starch in black beans will help your body to burn up to twenty-four percent more calories during the day.

Broccoli – Calcium and fiber help to break down fat in your body, and broccoli are loaded with both. A half-cup of raw broccoli has only twenty calories and four grams of fiber, so it is a veggie that will fill you up and keep you full for hours. It is also loaded with vitamin C, which gives a boost to your immune system as well as helping you to lose weight by burning fat faster and better.

Green Tea – This drink contains polyphenols that will activate the enzymes in your fat cells that will help to destroy them. One ingredient in green tea, EGCG, interacts with the pathways in your brain that control your appetite and will help to significantly reduce your body weight. Green tea also provides a boost of energy to your metabolism while promoting the process where fatty acids break down in your body and produce energy.

Spinach – One cup of raw spinach has four grams of fiber and only eight calories. When you eat spinach, it is broken down slowly in your body, so it will help to reduce your cravings for food since digesting spinach slows down the process of digestion.

SPECIAL CONCERNS FOR NUTRITION

Athletes who follow a well-planned vegan diet will not suffer a loss of performance, but they will need to pay special attention to ensure they get plenty of several necessary nutrients.

Vitamin B-12 – This vitamin is usually taken as a supplement by people who follow a vegan diet because it is needed for the proper function of your nervous system, and it is only found in animal foods.

Vitamin D – Besides going out in the sunlight so that your body can make its own Vitamin D, the best sources are fortified milk and many types of fish, neither of which are allowed on a vegan diet. You need Vitamin D for calcium absorption, bone health, and the function of your muscles. Many vegans choose to supplement with a vitamin.

Calcium – You need calcium for the health of your bones and for the proper functioning of your muscles, and you will be able to get good amounts of calcium from seeds, nuts, and leafy green veggies.

Iodine – Since most soils are now depleted of iodine, most plant foods do not provide enough of this vital nutrient. The most common way for people to get enough iodine in their diets is through using iodized salt because iodine is necessary for proper metabolism. If you are trying to limit your salt intake, you can also find a good source of iodine in seaweed.

Zinc – This mineral is not absorbed well when it comes to plants, and it is needed for the proper functioning of your immune system. You will absorb zinc from foods better when those foods are paired with foods that are high in protein. You should increase your consumption of pumpkin seeds or hemp seeds or consider using a vitamin supplement.

Iron – Since this mineral is used by your body to carry oxygen to your muscles, iron is a critically important nutrient for athletes. Muscles will not work if your body does not have an adequate supply of iron. Athletes will need to make sure that they eat enough leafy green veggies and beans. And since vitamin C helps your body absorb iron better, you should pair iron-rich foods with those high in vitamin C.

Omega-3s – These are fatty acids that are crucial to your health, and they must be consumed regularly. Omega-3s are especially beneficial for athletes because they will help to relieve inflammation. Only one type out of the three types of omega-3s is available in Plant-based foods, so you may want to consider a supplement.

Protein – Vegan athletes will need to make sure that they are getting enough protein in their diets. You will need protein for recovery after workouts and for muscle synthesis. And depending on the level of physical activity, your protein requirements may be even higher on some days than they are on others.

If you compare the three lists to each other, you will find that black beans, spinach, lentils, and almonds are all on two of the lists. It is helpful on the vegan diet for athletes to find foods that will help in more than one category to give you the best nutrition possible. When you are making your food plans, and creating your menus, keep in mind that everything that you eat matters. As an athlete, you cannot slack off in any area if you want to achieve the goals you have set for yourself. Nutrition is just as important as rigorous training.

The most effective meal plans will not restrict you to just a few foods but rather will open up endless possibilities for good tasting nutrition. Plant-based whole foods will promote good digestion, keep you feeling full, and boost your metabolism. Following a vegan diet will reduce your risk of developing a chronic disease as well as giving you more energy during workouts and faster recovery afterward.

CHAPTER 2: VEGAN NUTRITIONAL REQUIREMENTS

BASIC NUTRITIONAL NEEDS

Athletic performance can easily be supported or improved by following a vegan diet. Since plant foods are low in fat, high in carbs, and have rich levels of minerals, vitamins, and antioxidants, the vegan diet is the perfect solution for athletes of any level. A vegan diet is good not only for your heart but also for your performance and your recovery after performance. Animal fat, red meat, and products made from animals like milk and eggs are loaded with compounds that cause inflammation in your body. Working out causes inflammation in your body, but it's the good kind of inflammation. After a strenuous workout, you do not need a diet that will add more inflammation to your body. A vegan diet that is well-balanced is loaded with anti-inflammatory fats and lowers in the substances that cause inflammation.

The antioxidants that come from plants are particularly beneficial to athletes. While your intense workouts are doing amazing things for your body, they are also releasing more free radicals into your body. Free radicals are one-celled electrons that float around in your body when they are released as waste products during regular metabolic functions. Electrons like to be in pairs, so the free radicals float through the body seeking a pair to bond with. Their bond is usually made with a healthy cell, where they grab on and begin to deteriorate that healthy cell. The antioxidants that you get from plant foods will help to fight those free radicals and keep your body functioning at top form. This is especially true for the health of your muscles because muscle cells depend on one particular component of their makeup to create energy that is used during motion. Free radicals are known to destroy this particular component, leaving your cells without their energy centers. The muscle cells will then rely on a less efficient way to make energy that creates a buildup of lactic acid that leads to muscle fatigue.

The vegan diet will need to be carefully crafted in order to ensure that you are getting the nutrients that you need to fuel your training and performance. Consuming an adequate amount of protein can be challenging for athletes on the vegan diet. Protein is the building block that the body uses for creating muscle fiber. You will not be able to grow and maintain muscle mass unless you have an adequate intake of protein-based foods. And it is important to look for the vegan foods that contain all nine of the essential amino acids. You need amino acids to regulate your immune system and to build muscle. Of the twenty different amino acids, nine are not made by the body, and, unfortunately, these are the ones that your body needs the most. Buckwheat, soy, quorn, seitan, ezekial bread, and quinoa are the best single sources of all nine essential amino acids. But keep in mind that you do not need to limit yourself to these foods in order to get the nine essential amino acids that your body needs. The best method is to mix two protein foods to get all of the amino acids, such as mixing rice and beans together.

Another consideration for the vegan athlete is consuming enough calories during the day to fuel their bodies in the way they need to be fueled. Most vegans consume fewer calories than meat-eaters for the simple fact that animal products are more calorie-dense than plant products are. Consider the following table that shows the calorie counts for specific amounts of certain foods:

FOOD ITEM	CALORIES	PORTION SIZE
Steak	460	6 ounces
Chicken	407	6 ounces
Salmon	354	6 ounces
Deer	267	6 ounces
Lettuce	24	3 cups shredded
Tomatoes	31	One large
Mushrooms	38	Ten medium-sized
Broccoli	50	One medium stalk
Cauliflower	50	one-third of one head
Apples	95	One medium-sized
Oranges	63	Three small or two medium-sized
Bananas	105	one and one-half medium-sized

To consume four hundred sixty calories, you can either eat one six-ounce steak or fifteen large tomatoes. For three hundred fifty-four calories, you can eat one six-ounce salmon steak or forty-five cups of shredded lettuce. So the vegan athlete will need to ensure that they are consuming enough calories to maintain the performance level they wish to maintain. But a vegan diet for the athlete does not mean just giving up animal products. Too many people attempt the vegan diet and become deficient in their micronutrients because they do not balance their protein and caloric needs, and they end up eating too many refined carbs. When you are looking at foods for meals and planning your menus, you will want to think about your macronutrients (macros) and micronutrients (micros). Your micros are the minerals, antioxidants, phytonutrients, and vitamins you consume in your food. Macros are the three main food groups of carbs, protein, and dietary fat.

Your meal plan should always consider what you *are* eating as opposed to what you are *not* eating. Don't think of the foods that you left behind but rather think about all of the choices ahead of you. After all, beef is just beef, but there are so many veggies just waiting for you to try them. On the vegan athlete diet, healthy fats are important. You will find these in olives, avocados, seeds, and nuts. These foods are full of anti-inflammatory fats, and they will add to your overall caloric intake. Protein, like that found in oats, basmati rice, whole grains, peas, lentils, and beans, will combine with one another to provide you the nine essential amino acids that you need. And look for veggies and fruits in all the colors of the rainbow. The compounds that give veggies and fruits their color are also the compounds that give you minerals and vitamins.

MALE ATHLETES VS. FEMALE ATHLETES

It is important to recognize that the needs of the male athlete differ from the needs of the female athlete. Up until puberty, the male body and the female body have the same basic requirements for nutrition. But once puberty kicks in and the male body begins producing testosterone, the male will usually have significantly less body fat and larger muscle mass than the female body. Women have estrogen and body fat for a very basic reason: women carry babies. In ancient times when food might be scarce, and people would be forced to fast, it was important for the female body to be able to nourish the growing fetus, so women regularly carried more body fat than men did. Estrogen helps this by reducing the woman's ability to burn off energy after eating as well as men do, which results in more of their food intake being stored as fat in their bodies. Because of this, the female athlete will need to consume fewer calories than her male counterpart, and the mix of macros may need to be different.

Every meal that the female athlete eats should contain at least two veggies and fruits, and veggies are preferable to fruits because of the lower sugar content. For one day, the female athlete needs to consume at least seven servings of fruits and veggies. These will provide her with necessary carbs as well as total overall nutrients. The protein content of every meal should be between twenty-five and thirty-five percent. There are so many foods that are rich in protein that it should be easy to meet this requirement and not become bored with your food. When it comes to protein, the female athlete should try to rely less on soy products because soy contains compounds that mimic the effect of estrogen on the female body.

Dietary carbs should make up forty to sixty percent of the female athlete's overall food intake. It is important to keep away from consuming simple sugars like processed sweets and look to get your carb intake from complex carbs like brown rice, whole grain pasta, and whole-grain bread. If you find yourself running out of energy before the end of the day or the end of the workout, you may not be consuming enough carbs in your diet. And do not try to load up on carbs before an intense workout because your body will have more stamina if it is relying on fats and proteins to burn during effort.

Fat from natural sources is needed for ideal health. Female athletes, especially, should never be on a fat-free or low-fat diet. The fat in each meal should be between fifteen and twenty-five percent of the entire meal. Fat is essential because it not only contains vital nutrients, but the body needs some fat to be able to absorb other nutrients. You will get your dietary fat from nuts, seeds, avocados, olive oil, and nut butter.

This table shows the macros for different total calorie counts and how many calories should come from each macro.

CALORIES	CARBS 40%	PROTEIN 35%	FAT 25%
1500	600	525	375
1800	720	630	450
2000	800	700	500
2500	1000	875	625
3000	1200	1050	750

You will not need to strictly divide foods into each macro because nearly every food will contain more than one macro, like black beans, contain protein and carbs.

THE MALE ATHLETE

Men have different nutritional requirements than women do. Because of their higher testosterone levels, men have less body fat and more muscle mass than women do. Men will need to consume the right amounts of the right foods in order to remain in peak condition and have the stamina needed for their workouts.

Men will need to consume more calories than women will, and the largest macro they will be consuming is carbs. Carbs will provide fuel for the male athlete, and forty to fifty percent of their diet should be consumed as carbs. Look for the complex carbs of whole-grain bread and pasta, beans, and potatoes. Fat is the most energy-dense nutrient, and it contributes significantly to your energy levels. The fat consumption for a male athlete should be twenty to thirty percent of their total daily calories. And the protein ratio for the male athlete should be somewhere between thirty-five and forty percent. Here is what that would look like for various calories counts.

CALORIES	CARBS 40%	PROTEIN 40%	FAT 20%
2500	1000	1000	500
2800	1120	1120	560
3000	1200	1200	600
3500	1400	1400	700
4000	1600	1600	800
4500	1800	1800	900

Neither male nor female athletes should overlook their needs for hydration. No matter how healthy your diet is, you will not be able to function without adequate hydration. In fact, many times, dehydration mimics a nutrient shortage, making people think there is something wrong with their diet when the real problem is that they need more water. And consuming certain foods, like whole grains that soak up all the liquid in your stomach, will cause you to need an increase in your liquid intake.

If you make sure to eat good quality protein and fats, plenty of carbs, the right amount of calories for the needs of your body, and keep well-hydrated, then you will be able to navigate the vegan diet and still maintain your athletic performance.

CHAPTER 3: VEGAN FIT RECIPES

Vegan recipes do not need to be boring. There are so many different combinations of veggies, fruits, whole grains, beans, seeds, and nuts that you will be able to make unique meal plans for many months. These recipes contain the instructions along with the necessary ingredients and nutritional information.

ENERGIZING BREAKFASTS

A breakfast that has the right amount of protein and carbs will keep you feeling fuller longer and will help you to have the energy to make it through the day.

1. QUINOA & BANANA MEAL

Prep five min/cook twenty min/serves one

Ingredients:

- Dry quinoa, one half cup
- Almond milk, three-fourths cup
- Cinnamon, one teaspoon
- Vanilla extract, one teaspoon
- Peanut butter or almond butter, two tablespoons
- Bananas, two, sliced thinly
- Nutmeg, one half teaspoon

Method:

Set a small saucepan on the stove on top of medium heat. Pour in the almond milk, cinnamon, vanilla, nutmeg, and quinoa and mix all of the ingredients together. Bring this mixture to a rolling boil and then turn down the heat so that the mix can cook at a simmer for fifteen minutes. Set a lid on the pot while the mix simmers. When it looks like the quinoa has absorbed all of the liquid, take the saucepan off the heat and use a fork to fluff up the grains of quinoa. Spoon the cooked quinoa into a bowl and layer the sliced bananas and the peanut butter or almond butter on top. If you like, add another dash or two of cinnamon.

Nutrition info: Calories 315, carbs 57 grams, fat 6 grams, protein 9 grams, fiber ten grams

2. VEGAN OMELET WITH MUSHROOMS

Prep ten min/cook ten min/serves one

Ingredients:

Omelet

- Aquafaba, one-quarter cup*
- Salt, one half teaspoon
- Chickpea flour, one half cup
- Corn starch, one quarter tablespoon
- Tofu, extra firm, three ounces
- Nutritional yeast, one tablespoon
- Olive oil, one half teaspoon
- Turmeric powder, one half teaspoon

Garnish

- Scallion, one medium-sized sliced thinly
- Tomato, one-half medium-sized sliced thinly

Mushroom

- Button mushrooms, one ounce sliced
- Paprika, one half teaspoon
- Olive oil, one half teaspoon
- Soy sauce, one half teaspoon

Method:

Put all of the ingredients for the omelet except for the oil into a blender and blend until all of the ingredients are smooth. Place the oil for the mushrooms into a skillet on the stove over medium heat and add in the mushrooms. Fry them for five minutes, then stir in the soy sauce and paprika and mix well. Pour the omelet mixture from the blender on top of the fried mushrooms and let it fry for five minutes without being disturbed. While it is cooking, put the leftover oil into another skillet and start to heat it. After the omelet has cooked for five minutes, carefully flip it into the other pan and let it cook for five more minutes. Sprinkle the top of the cooked omelet with the scallions and lay the sliced tomatoes on the side.

Aquafaba is the water in which seeds of legumes like chickpeas are cooked. It acts just like egg whites and can also be used to make marshmallows and meringues for pies. Either keep the liquid from drained chickpeas or cook a batch of chickpeas and save the liquid. Then whip the liquid to make Aquafaba.

Nutrition info: Calories 205, carbs 22 grams, protein 17 grams, fat 10 grams, fiber 6 grams

3. PAPAYA AND MANGO WITH BABY SPINACH AND PEANUT BUTTER SAUCE

Prep ten min/serves one

Ingredients:

- Mango, one-half cup cut into cubes
- Papaya, one-half cup cut into cubes
- Almond milk, one half cup

- Baby spinach, one cup washed and dried
- Date, one with the stone removed
- Peanut butter, one tablespoon
- Sesame seeds, one teaspoon

Method:

Blend in a blender the almond milk, baby spinach, date, and peanut butter until everything is creamy and smooth. Place the cubes of papaya and mango in a serving bowl. Pour the blended sauce over the cubed fruit and top it with the sesame seeds.

4. CHICKPEA TOAST

Prep five min/cook thirty min/serves two

Ingredients:

- Whole wheat bread, four slices, can be gluten-free if needed
- Garlic, minced, one tablespoon
- Parsley, fresh and chopped, for garnish
- Paprika, ground, one half teaspoon
- Black olives, thinly sliced, for garnish
- Cinnamon, one teaspoon
- Garlic, minced, one tablespoon
- Chickpeas, pre-cooked, two cups
- Tomatoes, steamed and canned, one fifteen ounce can, chopped, save the juice
- Black pepper, one half teaspoon
- Olive oil, two tablespoons
- Salt, one quarter teaspoon
- Shallots, three small-sized, finely diced

Method:

Put the olive oil into a large skillet and set it on the stovetop on medium heat. When the oil is warm, then fry the shallots and garlic for five minutes. Stir in the salt, pepper, cinnamon, and paprika and mix it with the veggies well. Mix in the juice from the tomatoes with the tomatoes and turn down the heat so that this mix can simmer for five minutes. After five minutes, stir in the cooked chickpeas and then cook this mix for another five minutes while you stir often. Then spoon this mixture onto the toasted bread and use the black olives and parsley for garnish.

Nutrition per serving: Calories 423, 22 grams protein, 9 grams fiber, 15 grams fat, 45 grams carbs

5. MAPLE & NUTS

Prep five min/cook twenty min/serves four

Ingredients:

- Maple flavoring, one teaspoon
- Walnuts, one quarter cup
- Coconut flakes, unsweetened, one quarter cup
- Sunflower seeds, three tablespoons
- Cinnamon, one teaspoon
- Chia seeds, four tablespoons
- Pecans, one quarter cup
- Almond milk, one third cup

Method:

The walnuts, sunflower seeds, and pecans will need to be crushed into fine bits. Then place a medium-sized saucepan on the stove over medium-high heat and pour in the crushed nuts. Add in the coconut flakes, almond milk, cinnamon, and maple flavoring and mix all of the ingredients together well. When the mixture reaches a boil, then turn the heat down and allow it all to simmer for thirty minutes. You will need to stir this often so that the chia seeds do not stick to the bottom of the pan. When you serve it, sprinkle on a bit of cinnamon.

Nutrition info: Calories 374, 10 grams protein, 35 grams fat, 4 grams carbs, 10 grams fiber

6. SCRAMBLED TOFU

Prep ten min/cook twenty min/serves one

Ingredients:

- Black pepper, one half teaspoon
- Salt, one half teaspoon
- Tofu, firm, four ounces
- Cumin, ground, one half teaspoon
- Nutritional yeast, one half teaspoon
- Paprika, one half teaspoon
- Turmeric, one half teaspoon
- Water, one half tablespoon
- Cherry tomatoes, one-half cup, cut into quarters
- Olive oil, one tablespoon
- Red onion, one-half medium-sized sliced thinly
- Mushrooms, one-half cup, washed, dried, and finely chopped
- Soy sauce, one half tablespoon

Method:

Place a large skillet on the stovetop and pour in the olive oil. Place the sliced onion into the heated olive oil and fry it for five minutes. Add in the soy sauce and the sliced mushrooms and cook this for another five minutes. While these are cooking crumble the tofu into little pebble-sized pieces. Pour the crumbled tofu and the cherry tomatoes into the skillet with the salt, pepper, cumin, paprika, water, and turmeric and cook this for another eight minutes. Sprinkle the nutritional yeast on top and serve.

Nutrition info: Calories 561, 21 grams fat, 22 grams fiber, 34 grams protein, 69 grams carbs

7. VEGAN TACOS

Prep fifteen min/cook fifteen min/serves one

Ingredients:

- Black pepper, one half teaspoon
- Olive oil, one half tablespoon
- Firm tofu, crumbled, three ounces
- Cumin, one half teaspoon
- Nutritional yeast, one tablespoon
- Salt, one half teaspoon
- Turmeric powder, one half teaspoon
- Avocado, one half sliced thinly
- Cilantro, fresh, one tablespoon chopped
- Lime juice, one tablespoon
- Red onion, medium-sized, one fourth sliced thinly
- Tomato, medium-sized, one fourth sliced thinly
- Corn tortillas, three

Method:

Place the olive oil in a large skillet over medium heat and add in the tofu, frying it for five minutes while you stir occasionally. Mix in the turmeric, salt, pepper, and cumin and fry the tofu for three more minutes. Wrap the corn tortillas in a damp paper towel and microwave them on high for fifteen seconds to warm them. Divide the seasoned tofu onto the three tortillas and top with equal amounts of the cilantro, avocado, red onion, and tomato. Drizzle lime juice and the nutritional yeast over the top and serve.

Calories 428, 25 grams fat, 69 grams carbs, 20 grams protein, 18 grams fiber

8. POTATO HASH WITH MUSHROOMS AND ASPARAGUS

Prep ten min/cook twenty min/serves four

Ingredients:

- Chives, one-half cup for garnish
- Mushrooms, button, one half cup
- Roasted red peppers, one-half cup rinsed
- Potatoes, one pound, peeled, boiled, and cooled
- Parsley, chopped, one-quarter cup for garnish
- Sage, dried, one teaspoon
- Olive oil, three tablespoons
- Black pepper, one half teaspoon
- Onion, one small chopped large
- Garlic, minced, one tablespoon
- Asparagus, one pound, trimmed, cut in one half inch long chunks
- Shallot, one chopped
- Salt, one half teaspoon

Method:

Chop the precooked potatoes into chunks that are bite-sized. Place one tablespoon of the olive oil in a large skillet on the stovetop and warm it over medium heat. Drop in the asparagus, shallots, mushrooms, and garlic into the hot oil and fry them together for five minutes while you stir this mixture often. Now pour in the leftover two tablespoons of the olive oil and stir in the onions and the potato chunks and mix everything together well. Cook all of this for five to ten minutes while you stir it occasionally, cooking just until the potatoes are browned. Then mix in the sage, red pepper, pepper, and salt and mix thoroughly and then cook it for one more minute. Serve the mix with the parsley, and the chives sprinkled on top for garnish.

Nutrition info: Calories 239, 5 grams fiber, 30 grams carbs, 11 grams fat, 6 grams protein

9. LENTIL AND BROCCOLI CUTLETS

Prep ten min/cook fifteen min/serves five

Ingredients:

- Panko bread crumbs, one quarter cup
- Broccoli, florets, two cups chopped into tiny bits
- Salt, one half teaspoon
- Cumin, powdered, one teaspoon
- Onion powder, one teaspoon
- Olive oil, two tablespoons
- Cayenne pepper, one half teaspoon
- Basil, dried, one teaspoon
- Lentils, red, one cup, soaked overnight and drained
- Nutmeg, one half teaspoon

Method:

Drain the water off the lentils and then mash them until you have a creamy, smooth mixture. Pour in the chopped bits of broccoli and mix these together well. Then put in the nutmeg, basil, cayenne pepper, onion powder, cumin, and salt and mix until all of these are well mixed into the lentil mash. Divide this batter into ten portions that are close to equal in size. Place a large skillet on the stovetop over medium-high heat and heat the olive oil. While the oil is heating flatten, the portions of batter slightly and coat them with the bread crumbs. Fry the portions in the hot olive oil for five minutes on each side.

Nutrition info per two cutlets: Calories 169, 12 grams fiber, 1 gram fat, 30 grams carbs, 11 grams protein

10. MATCHA SMOOTHIE BOWL

Prep five min/serves one

Ingredients:

- Banana, one medium-sized chopped small
- Goji berries, dried, two tablespoons
- Mint, fresh, four tablespoons washed, dried, and stems removed
- Matcha green tea powder, one half teaspoon
- Persimmon, chopped, one
- Sesame seeds, one teaspoon
- Water, one cup

Method:

Place in a blender the matcha powder, water, banana, and half of the mint leaves and blend all of this together until it is smooth and creamy. Pour the mixture into a bowl and top with the remainder of the mint leaves along with the sesame seeds, goji berries, and chopped persimmons.

Nutrition info: Calories 289, 2 grams fat, 12 grams fiber, 69 grams carbs, 5 grams protein

11. BREAKFAST MILLET WITH APPLES

Prep five min/cook ten min/serves one

Ingredients:

- Almond milk, one cup
- Dates, two, pit removed and sliced thinly
- Millet, one-half cup rinsed well
- Salt, one quarter teaspoon
- Turmeric powder, one half teaspoon
- Vanilla extract, one half teaspoon
- Apple, one medium-sized, washed off and chopped
- Sunflower oil, one half teaspoon
- Maple syrup, one tablespoon

Method:

Place a medium-sized saucepan on the stovetop and pour in the almond milk, millet, dates, and vanilla extract. Cook this over medium heat while you stir occasionally for five minutes. While this is cooking, place the olive oil into a small skillet over medium heat and cook the apples when the oil is warm, stirring often, for five minutes. When the millet has cooked for ten minutes, then remove it from the heat and mix in the salt and the turmeric. Pour the millet into a serving bowl and add the fried apples on top of the millet. Drizzle the maple syrup on top and serve.

Nutrition info: Calories 405, 57 grams carbs, 7 grams fiber, 21 grams protein, 11 grams fat

12. BANANA FRENCH TOAST

Prep ten min/cook twenty-five min/serves three

Ingredients:

- Bread, whole wheat, one loaf
- Almond milk, one half cup
- Bananas, two sliced thin
- Vanilla extract, one teaspoon
- Nutmeg, one half teaspoon
- Coconut oil, two tablespoons

Method:

In a shallow bowl, mix together the nutmeg, vanilla extract, and the almond milk. Lay each slice of bread in the milk mixture for a few seconds until each slice is well-coated. Place the coconut oil in a large skillet over high heat and fry the dipped slices of bread in the coconut oil for five minutes. Place the cooked slices of bread on serving plates and top with the sliced bananas.

Nutrition info per serving: Calories 220, 2 grams fat, 49 grams carbs, 2 grams protein, 4 grams fiber

13. HEMP PORRIDGE WITH PEARS AND BLUEBERRIES

Prep five min/cook five min/serves one

Ingredients:

- Almond milk, one cup
- Blueberries, one half cup
- Hemp seeds, one half tablespoons

- Pear, one medium-sized sliced
- Porridge oats, one half cup

Method:

In a medium-sized saucepan over a medium heat pour in the porridge and the almond milk. Bring the mix to a boil and then turn down the heat and let the porridge simmer for five minutes. Spoon the porridge into a bowl and top it with the blueberries, hemp seeds, and pears and serve.

Nutrition info: Calories 463, 17 grams protein, 13 grams fiber, 78 grams carbs, 11 grams fat

14. TOFU SCRAMBLE WITH ONIONS AND PEPPERS

Prep five min/cook five min/serves two

Ingredients:

- Cilantro, fresh, one third cup
- Onion, diced, one quarter cup
- Salt, one half teaspoon
- Black pepper, one teaspoon
- Olive oil, one tablespoon
- Tofu, firm, one cup
- Red bell pepper, one diced
- Nutritional yeast, one quarter cup

Method:

Place the olive oil in a medium-sized skillet on the stovetop over medium heat and add in the onions and the peppers. Fry them for five minutes while you stir them often. While the onions and peppers are frying mash the tofu in a bowl and mix in the pepper and the salt. Pour the mashed tofu into the skillet and mix everything well. Cook this mixture for five more minutes while you stir it occasionally. When this mix has cooked for five more minutes, then mix in the nutritional yeast and the cilantro. Mix this in well and then serve.

Nutrition info per serving: Calories 369, 7 grams fiber, 26 grams fat, 20 grams protein, 14 grams carbs

15. MUSHROOM SANDWICH WITH LEAFY GREENS

Prep forty-five min/cook forty-five min/serves four

Ingredients:

- Tomato, one large sliced into four slices
- Arugula or spinach, two cups, cleaned and chopped and cooked as desired
- Black pepper, one teaspoon
- Garlic, minced, one tablespoon
- Mayonnaise, vegan, one quarter cup
- Salt, one half teaspoon
- Lemon juice, one teaspoon
- Olive oil, one tablespoon
- Portobello mushroom caps, four large with gills removed
- Eggplant, four thin slices

Method:

In a small-sized bowl, blend together the mayonnaise, minced garlic, and the lemon juice. Use the olive oil to coat the mushroom caps and the slices of the eggplant and then grill these in a large-sized skillet over high heat for five minutes, two-and-one-half minutes on each side. Lay each mushroom cap on a serving plate and lay one slice of grilled eggplant on top of each mushroom cap. Drop one teaspoon of the mayonnaise on top of the slices of eggplant and then top this with one slice of tomato. Serve each mushroom cap sandwich with a side of leafy greens.

Nutrition info per serving: Calories 289, 10 grams protein, 6 grams fiber, 11 grams fat, 15 grams carbs

1. MUSHROOM RISOTTO WITH CAULIFLOWER RICE

Prep twenty min/cook thirty min/serves six

Ingredients:

- Black pepper, one teaspoon
- Salt, one half teaspoon
- Parsley, dried, two tablespoons
- Nutritional yeast, one half cup
- Aquafaba, one cup
- Cauliflower, riced, four cups
- Vegetable broth, two cups divided
- Mushrooms, button, one cup sliced thin
- Shallot, one large, minced
- Onion, one small, well diced
- Garlic, minced, four tablespoons
- Olive oil, three tablespoons

Method:

Place the olive oil in a large skillet on the stovetop over a medium heat and pour in the onion, garlic, and shallot when the oil is hot. Fry these together for five minutes, stirring occasionally. Pour in one of the cups of vegetable broth and the sliced mushrooms and mix them in well, and then cook all of this for five more minutes. Add in the other cup of vegetable broth along with the riced cauliflower and mix it in well. Stir this mixture often while you cook it for ten more minutes. Then blend in the pepper, salt, parsley, aquafaba, and the nutritional yeast and turn the burner on the stove to low heat. Let this simmer for ten to fifteen minutes while you stir it sometimes. The mixture will thicken as it cooks.

Nutrition info per serving: Calories 297, 7 grams protein, 26 grams fat, 8 grams fiber, 8 grams carbs

2. ZUCCHINI LASAGNA

Prep twenty min/cook one hour/serves nine

Ingredients:

- Basil, finely chopped fresh, one half of one cup
- Zucchini, three medium sliced paper-thin from end to end
- Black pepper, one teaspoon
- Marinara sauce, one twenty-eight-ounce jar
- Lemon juice, two tablespoons
- Nutritional yeast, two tablespoons
- Olive oil, one tablespoon
- Water, one half of one cup
- Oregano, dried, two teaspoons
- Salt, one half teaspoon
- Tofu, extra firm, one sixteen ounce block drained and pressed for ten minutes
- Parsley, fresh, chopped fine, one-half cup for garnish

Method:

Heat the oven to 350. Cut the block of tofu into small chunks and place it into a medium-sized mixing bowl. Cream into the tofu the salt, pepper, water, oregano, basil, lemon juice, olive oil, and the nutritional yeast. Keep on blending the ingredients together until it looks like a smooth, creamy paste. Grease a thirteen by a nine-inch baking dish with spray oil. Cover the bottom of the baking dish with one cup of the marinara and use a spatula to move it around. Lay thin slices of the zucchini over the spread-out marinara. Drop small drops of the tofu mix on top of the zucchini noodles and spread it out gently. Pour some extra marinara sauce on top of this and add in more zucchini noodles and more tofu mix. Continue layering the three ingredients until all of them are completely used. The very top layer should be a thin layer of the marinara sauce. Place aluminum foil over the baking dish and bae it in the hot oven for forty-five minutes. Then remove the aluminum foil and let the dish bake for fifteen more minutes. Immediately upon removing it from the oven, cut the lasagna into nine equally sized squares. Sprinkle the fresh parsley over the top and serve.

Nutrition info per square: Calories 338, 10 grams carbs, 5 grams protein, 6 grams fiber, 34 grams fat

3. MEDITERRANEAN SPAGHETTI SQUASH

Prep forty min/cook thirty min/serves two

Ingredients:

- Avocado oil, two tablespoons
- Thyme, dried, one half teaspoon
- Spinach, fresh or frozen chopped finely, one cup
- Cherry tomatoes, eight, cut in three slices
- Spaghetti squash, one large
- Chickpeas, one-third of one cup, drained and rinsed
- Salt, one half teaspoon
- Garlic, minced, one tablespoon
- Marjoram, dried, one teaspoon
- Rosemary, dried, one teaspoon

- Nutritional yeast, two tablespoons
- Onion, red, one-quarter of one cup sliced thinly

Method:

Heat the oven to 400. Rinse off the skin of the spaghetti squash and dry it well. Cut the spaghetti squash in half from one end to the other. Dig out the seeds with a spoon and throw them away. Use one tablespoon of the avocado oil to lightly coat the inside half of the squash and lay them facing down on a cookie sheet that has been lined with parchment paper or aluminum foil. Poke five or six holes into the skin of the squash to let the steam vent out. Bake the spaghetti squash for thirty minutes in the hot oven. After thirty minutes, remove the squash from the oven and use a fork to scrape the flesh out of the squash. The flesh will come out in long strings that look like spaghetti. Put this spaghetti into a medium-sized bowl and set it off to the side. Set a large skillet on the stovetop over a medium heat and add the other tablespoon of the avocado oil. Put in the garlic and the onion and stir them occasionally while cooking them for five minutes. Then mix in the chickpeas along with the marjoram, tomatoes, rosemary, and thyme and cook everything together for five more minutes. Blend in the spinach, salt, and spaghetti squash and cook for five minutes while you stir gently and occasionally. Sprinkle the nutritional yeast over the top and serve immediately.

Nutrition info per serving: Calories 272, 10 grams fat, 11 grams fiber, 14 grams carbs, 11 grams protein

4. CREAMY CURRY NOODLES

Prep ten min/cook ten min/serves four

Ingredients:

Creamy Curry Sauce

- Apple cider vinegar, two tablespoons
- Water, one-quarter of one cup
- Avocado oil, two tablespoons
- Turmeric, ground, one teaspoon

- Black pepper, one half teaspoon

- Tahini, one-quarter of one cup

- Coriander, ground, one and one half teaspoons

- Cumin, ground, one teaspoon

- Salt, one teaspoon

- Curry powder, two teaspoons

- Ginger, ground, one quarter teaspoon

Noodle Bowl

- Cilantro, fresh, chopped small, one half of one cup

- Bell pepper, red, one cleaned and diced

- Zucchini noodles, one sixteen ounce pack

- Carrots, two, peeled and cut in julienne strips

- Kale, two cups packed

- Cauliflower, one half of one head chopped small

Method:

Cover the zucchini noodles with two cups of boiling water in a medium-sized bowl and set them off to the side. After leaving the noodles in the water for five minutes, drain off the water and place the noodles back into the bowl. Prep all of the veggies and then toss them into the bowl with the noodles. Toss the ingredients in the bowl gently, but well. Divide the leaves of kale onto four serving plates. Mix together the list of ingredients for the Creamy Curry Sauce and blend them until they are smooth and creamy. When the sauce is well mixed, then pour it over the ingredients in the bowl and toss the ingredients well until all are covered with the sauce. Then divide the noodles over the kale on the four plates and serve.

Nutrition info per serving: Calories 192, 12 grams fiber, 15 grams fat, 16 grams carbs, 5 grams protein

Prep ten min/cook twenty min/serves four

Ingredients:

Garnish

- Cilantro, chopped, one-quarter of one cup
- Green onion, diced, one half of one cup

Masala Seasoning

- Black pepper, one half teaspoon
- Turmeric, one quarter teaspoon
- Chili powder, ground, one half teaspoon
- Tomato puree, one half of one cup
- Garam masala, one quarter teaspoon
- Salt, one half teaspoon
- Garlic, minced, one tablespoon
- Olive oil, two tablespoons
- Ginger, ground, two teaspoons

Veggies

- Cauliflower, one cup in small pieces
- Mushrooms, sliced one half of one cup
- Green beans, three-fourths of one cup

Method:

Heat the oven to 400. Place the rack in the oven in the middle. Use aluminum foil or parchment paper to completely cover a baking sheet. Chop the veggies if they are not already chopped. Use a medium-sized bowl to mix together the chili powder, ginger, garam masala, garlic, pepper, salt, and the tomato puree, making sure the ingredients are all mixed together well. Then mix in the olive oil. Place the chopped veggies into this mixture and mix them in well. Then place the coated veggies onto the covered baking sheet in one single layer. Roast the veggies in the heated oven for thirty to forty minutes or until the veggies are cooked to the manner in which you like them.

Nutrition info per serving: Calories 105, 3 grams protein, 15 grams fiber, 7 grams fat, 10 grams carbs

6. KOREAN PSEUDO BEEF BOWL

Prep fifteen min/cook ten min/serves two

Ingredients:

- Broccoli, cooked, one cup
- Tofu, firm, pressed and drained, baked, one cup
- Sesame oil, two tablespoons
- Cauliflower rice, two cups
- Tamari, one tablespoon
- Mushrooms, cooked, one half of one cup
- Sesame seeds, two teaspoons
- Scallions, chopped, one half cup

Method:

Put the sesame oil into a large skillet and set the skillet on the stovetop over medium heat. Place into the hot oil the baked tofu, cooked cauliflower, cooked mushrooms, and the cooked broccoli. Mix all of the ingredients together thoroughly and keep stirring often until they are heated throughout, cooking for about fifteen minutes. Blend in the sesame seeds and the tamari and mix them in well. Then divide this mixture between two bowls and top each bowl with the chopped scallions and eat.

Nutrition info per bowl: Calories 247, 9 grams fiber, 13 grams fat, 9 grams carbs, 18 grams protein

7. LENTILS WITH CAULIFLOWER AND SWEET POTATO

Prep twenty min/cook thirty-five min/serves four

Ingredients:

- Sweet potato, one large, scrub the skin and cut it into small chunks
- Cauliflower, one head, cut into small florets
- Garam masala, one tablespoon
- Olive oil, three tablespoons
- Garlic, minced, two tablespoons
- Lentils, one cup
- Ginger, ground, one teaspoon
- Dijon mustard, one teaspoon
- Lime juice, two tablespoons
- Carrots, two
- Red cabbage, one quarter
- Coriander, one half cup

Method:

Heat the oven to 400 degrees. Place the cauliflower florets and the sweet potato chunks into a medium-sized bowl and sprinkle on the garam masala and half of the oil, tossing the veggies to coat them well. Lay the veggies out on a large baking sheet and sprinkle them with the minced garlic. Roast the veggies for thirty to thirty-five minutes or until they are completely cooked. While the veggies are roasting, put the lentils into a medium-sized saucepan with two cups of water. Set the saucepan on the stovetop over a medium heat and bring it to a rolling boil. Then turn down the heat and let the lentils simmer for twenty to thirty minutes or until the lentils are just turning soft. Drain off the water from the lentils. Take the roasted veggies from the oven and place them in a large-sized bowl, then add in the lentils and mix everything together well. Wash and grate the carrots and shred the cabbage finely. Add the coriander into the bowl of lentils with the carrots and the cabbage and mix them in well. Drizzle the lime juice over the bowl and then divide the mixture between four bowls and serve.

Nutrition info per bowl: Calories 350, 13 grams fiber, 15 grams protein, 41 grams carbs, 11 grams fat

8. ROASTED PEPPER PASTA SALAD

Prep thirty min/serves four

Ingredients:

- Whole wheat penne, six ounces
- Roasted red peppers, one jar seventeen ounces, rinse and slice
- Black pepper, one half teaspoon
- Scallions, one-half cup chopped finely
- Salt, one half teaspoon
- Capers, two tablespoons chopped finely
- Garlic, minced, one tablespoon
- Soy yogurt, plain nonfat, two tablespoons
- Lemon juice, two teaspoons
- Olive oil, one tablespoon
- Basil, dried, two tablespoons

Method:

Cook the whole wheat pasta the way the package instructs and then drain it and rinse it. Mix together in a small size bowl the capers, scallions, and half of the roasted red peppers. In another small bowl mix together well the soy yogurt, pepper, salt, garlic, lemon juice, oil, basil, and the other half of the roasted red peppers. Add the cooked noodles to the first bowl of ingredients and toss them together lightly, but well. Pour on top the ingredients of the second bowl and repeat the process.

Nutrition info per serving: Calories 258, 6 grams fiber, 16 grams protein, 39 grams carbs, 5 grams fat

9. WHITE BEAN BOLOGNESE

Prep forty min/cook fifteen min/serves four

Ingredients:

- Nutritional yeast, one half cup
- Fettuccini, whole wheat, eight ounces cooked
- White beans, one fourteen ounce can drain and rinse
- Parsley, fresh, chopped, one-quarter cup divided
- Tomatoes, diced, one fourteen ounce can
- Olive oil, two tablespoons
- Balsamic vinegar, one half cup
- Garlic, minced, three tablespoons
- Salt, one half teaspoon
- Celery, chopped, one quarter cup
- Carrot, chopped, one quarter cup
- Onion, one small chopped

Method:

Place the olive oil in a large skillet on the stovetop over a medium heat. Stir in the garlic, onion, carrots, and celery and fry them for ten minutes while you stir it occasionally. Add in the salt and stir well. Pour in the balsamic vinegar and bring the mixture to a boil, letting it boil for five minutes. Mix in the tomatoes, white beans, and two tablespoons of the chopped parsley into the skillet and stir often while the mixture simmers for five minutes. Spoon the cooked pasta into four bowls, dividing evenly. Use the sauce mix in the skillet to cover the pasta, dividing it evenly among the four bowls. Top each of the bowls with the nutritional yeast and the remainder of the parsley.

Nutrition info per bowl: Calories 442, 68 grams carbs, 18 grams protein, 11 grams fat, 13 grams fiber

10. VEGETABLES AND FARRO

Prep fifteen min/cook forty min/serves four

Ingredients:

Red Wine Vinaigrette

- Red pepper flakes, crushed, one quarter teaspoon
- Olive oil, one quarter cup
- Black pepper, one teaspoon
- Balsamic vinegar, three tablespoons
- Salt, one half teaspoon
- Lemon juice, two tablespoons
- Oregano, dried, one tablespoon
- Garlic, minced, one tablespoon

Farro and Veggies

- Farro, two cups cooked
- Butter lettuce, one head torn
- Olive oil, two tablespoons
- Red bell pepper, one diced
- Garlic, minced, two tablespoons
- Paprika, one tablespoon
- Balsamic vinegar, two tablespoons
- Dill, dried, one tablespoon

- Black pepper, one teaspoon

- Oregano, dried, one tablespoon

- Rosemary, one teaspoon

- Salt, one half teaspoon

- Red potatoes, one pound cut in wedges

Red onion, cucumber, green and/or black olives for serving

Method:

Heat the oven to 425. In a medium-sized bowl, mix together the paprika, rosemary, salt, pepper, oregano, balsamic vinegar, dill, garlic, and one tablespoon of the olive oil. Place the bell peppers and the potatoes in a thirteen by nine-inch baking dish and cover them with the mixed seasonings that you just mixed up. Bake the veggies in the hot oven for forty-five minutes. While the veggies are in the oven baking mix together well in a small-sized bowl all of the ingredients for the vinaigrette. Divide up the lettuce between four serving bowls and cover the lettuce with the cooked farro and then add on the mixture of roasted veggies. Drizzle all of the bowls with the mixed vinaigrette and serve the bowls with the cucumber, onion, and olives on the side.

Nutrition info per bowl: Calories 782, 6 grams fiber, 19 grams carbs, 4 grams fat, 10 grams protein

11. MUSHROOM AND BROWN RICE RISOTTO

Prep twenty min/cook thirty min/serves six

Ingredients:

- Black pepper, one teaspoon

- Olive oil, two tablespoons

- Salt, one half teaspoon

- Marjoram, one teaspoon

- Parsley, dried, one tablespoon

- Brown rice, four cups

- Garlic, minced, two tablespoons

- Vegetable broth, two cups divided

- Mushrooms, button, one cup, sliced thin

- Onion, one small, well diced

- Shallot, one large, minced

Method:

Put the olive oil in a large skillet on the stovetop over a medium heat. Put in the skillet the garlic, onion, and the shallot and fry them together for five minutes. Pour into the veggies one cup of the vegetable broth along with the mushrooms and cook all of this for five more minutes. Then add in the other cup of the vegetable broth with the brown rice. Cook all of this mixture for ten minutes while you stir it often to keep it well blended. Blend in the parsley, pepper, and the salt and then turn the heat under the skillet to low and let the mixture simmer for fifteen minutes or until you feel the rice is completely cooked.

Nutrition info per serving: Calories 297, 7 grams protein, 8 grams carbs, 26 grams fat, 10 grams fiber

12. EGGPLANT CASSEROLE

Prep fifteen min/cook thirty min/serves six

Ingredients:

- Eggplant, one medium

- Olive oil, two tablespoons

- Tomato soup, one can

- Shallots, one-quarter cup chopped fine

- Rosemary, one teaspoon

- Celery, one-half cup chopped fine

- Salt, one half teaspoon

- Onion, chopped, one quarter cup

Method:

Heat the oven to 375. Wash and peel the eggplant and then dice the flesh into cubes that are bite-size. Drop the cubes of eggplant into a pot of boiling water and cook them for five minutes, and then drain the eggplant well. Lay the eggplant into a nine by nine-inch square baking pan. Place the olive oil into a large skillet on the stovetop over a medium heat and fry the shallots, celery, and onions for five minutes. Pour the tomato soup into the cooked veggies and cook this mix for five minutes while you stir it often. Pour all of this mixture into the baking dish with the eggplant and bake it for thirty minutes.

Nutrition info preserving: Calories 267, 9 grams fat, 6 grams fiber, 19 grams carbs, 13 grams protein

13. MINI PITAS WITH BLACK BEANS

Prep one hour/cook thirty min/serves eight

Ingredients:

Sauce

- Tomatoes, two chopped

- Mini whole-wheat pita breads, sixteen

- Dill, fresh, two tablespoons chopped

- Red onion, one half thin sliced

- Garlic, minced, one tablespoon

- Black pepper, one teaspoon

- Romaine lettuce, four leaves shred

- Lemon juice, one tablespoon

- Parsley, fresh, one quarter cup chop

- Cucumber, one half thin sliced

- Salt, one half teaspoon

Black Beans

- Black beans, canned drained and rinsed, two cups

- Paprika, smoked, one quarter teaspoon

- Black pepper, one teaspoon

- Olive oil, one quarter cup

- Lemon juice, two tablespoons

- Garlic powder, two teaspoons

- Lemon zest, one tablespoon

- Cumin, ground, one teaspoon

- Coriander, ground, three quarters teaspoon

Method:

Blend together in a medium-sized bowl the black beans with the garlic powder, lemon zest, lemon juice, olive oil, cumin, pepper, and the coriander. Set this bowl into the refrigerator and let it steep there for one hour. While it is in the refrigerator mix together in another bowl, the parsley, garlic, salt, pepper, dill, and lemon juice. Place this bowl in the refrigerator and get the first bowl out of the refrigerator. Place a large skillet on the stovetop and pour in the bean mix and bring it to a rolling boil. Turn down the heat and let the mixture simmer until almost all of the liquid is cooked off while you stir it often. Use the sauce mixture and the black bean mixture to fill the pitas and serve.

Nutrition info per one pita: Sauce Calories 300, 56 grams carbs, 5 grams fiber, 13 grams protein, 5 grams fat/Beans Calories 154, 5 grams fiber, 9 grams protein, 16 grams fat, 10 grams carbs

Prep fifteen min/cook thirty min/serves four

Ingredients:

- Parsley, fresh chopped, one third cup
- Lemons, three, sliced thin
- Green olives, one cup
- Red onion, one half minced
- Vegetable broth, two and one half cups
- Rice, brown or wild, one cup
- Garlic, minced, two tablespoons
- Oregano, dried, one teaspoon
- Olive oil, two tablespoons
- Rosemary, one teaspoon
- Black pepper, one teaspoon
- Marjoram, one teaspoon
- Salt, one half teaspoon

Method:

Put the olive oil in a large skillet and add in the garlic and onion and fry them for five minutes. Pour into the skillet the vegetable broth, pepper, salt, onion, rice, oregano, marjoram, and rosemary. Mix all of those ingredients together well and let them simmer for thirty minutes until the rice is completely cooked. Top the individual servings with the olives, fresh parsley, and slices of the lemon.

Nutrition info per serving: Calories 903, 11 grams fiber, 48 grams protein, 55 grams fat, 54 grams carbs

15. BLACK BEAN SWEET POTATO RICE BOWL

Prep thirty min/serves four

Ingredients:

- Sweet chili sauce, two tablespoons
- Long grain rice, three-fourths cup uncooked
- Black beans, one fifteen ounce can drain and rinse
- Oregano, one teaspoon
- Kale, fresh, four cups chopped
- Turmeric, one teaspoon
- Red onion, one fine chop
- Olive oil, three tablespoons
- Garlic salt, one quarter teaspoon
- Water, one and one half cups
- Sweet potato, two peeled and chopped into bite-sized pieces
- Celery, one-half cup chopped

Method:

Add the garlic salt and the rice to two cups of boiling water in a medium-sized saucepan and cook it for twenty minutes. While the rice is cooking, put the olive oil in a large skillet on the stovetop over medium heat and cook the sweet potato for eight minutes while you stir it often. After the sweet potato has cooked, then mix in the onion, oregano, turmeric, celery, kale, and the beans and let all of this cook for five more minutes. Mix the chili sauce into the cooked rice and then add that to the potato mixture in the skillet and serve.

Nutrition info per two cups: Calories 453, 10 grams protein, 74 grams carbs, 8 grams fiber, 11 grams fat

FAT BURNING RECIPES

1. WHITE BEAN AND FARRO VEGGIE BURGER

Prep thirty min/cook fifty min/serves four

Ingredients:

- Farro, three-fourths cup uncooked
- Water, three cups
- Vegetable broth, one teaspoon
- Cannellini beans, one fifteen ounce can drained (save the liquid)
- Onion, one medium finely diced
- Mushrooms, one cup finely chopped
- Carrots, two medium washed and grated
- Walnuts, chopped, one fourth cup
- Oregano, dried, one teaspoon
- Chives, dried, two tablespoons
- Old-fashioned oats, one third cup
- Bread crumbs, whole grain, one half cup
- Rosemary, one teaspoon
- Black pepper, one half teaspoon
- Turmeric, one half teaspoon
- Olive oil, three tablespoons
- Whole-grain buns, ten
- Lettuce leaves, eight
- Tomatoes, three medium sliced

- Avocados, two sliced

Method:

Put the vegetable broth and the water into a medium-sized saucepan and add the farro. Bring this to a boil over medium-high heat, then lower the heat to medium and cook the farro for forty minutes and then drain. Pour the cannellini beans into a medium-sized bowl and mash them. Mix in the rosemary, turmeric, black pepper, bread crumbs, oats, chives, oregano, walnuts, carrots, onion, mushrooms, and the cooked farro. Mix all of these ingredients together well and then add two or three tablespoons of the saved bean liquid so that the mix will hold together. Set the bowl in the refrigerator and let it chill for one hour. use one-half cup of the bean mix to make a patty, making four patties, and cook them in the olive oil. Fry them for six minutes on each side. Repeat this in groups of four, adding more olive oil as needed. Serve each of the patties with one bun, lettuce, avocado slices, and tomato slices.

Nutrition per serving: Calories 354, 15 grams fat, 11 grams fiber, 50 grams carbs, 11 grams protein

2. LOADED SWEET POTATOES

Prep fifteen min/cook fifty min/serves six

Ingredients:

- Sweet potatoes, six
- Zucchini, one medium
- Onion, one large
- Bell peppers, two
- Tomato, one
- Avocados, two
- Black beans, one fifteen-ounce can
- Garlic, minced, two tablespoons
- Cumin, one tablespoon

- Chili powder, one teaspoon

- Cayenne pepper, one half teaspoon

- Black pepper, one half teaspoon

- Salsa, six tablespoons divided

- Olive oil, two tablespoons

Method:

Heat the oven to 375. Scrub the skin of the sweet potatoes. Lay the sweet potatoes on a cookie sheet and bake them for forty minutes. While the potatoes are baking, wash the other veggies and dice all of them individually. Fry the garlic and onions in the olive oil for five minutes, then stir in the zucchini and peppers and cook for five more minutes. Stir in the spices and mix together well. Drain the liquid off the beans and add them to the skillet, mixing well. Slice the sweet potatoes in half the long way and mash the insides in the skin slightly to make it soft. Then add the veggie mix to all four halves. Top the potatoes with the salsa, avocado, and diced tomato.

Nutrition per half: Calories 316, 14 grams fiber, 50 grams carbs, 9 grams protein, 11 grams fat

3. CURRIED CHICKPEAS IN PEANUT COCONUT SAUCE

Prep fifteen min/cook twenty min/serves four

Ingredients:

- Olive oil, one tablespoon

- Onion, one half chopped

- Chickpeas, one fifteen-ounce can drain and rinse

- Diced tomatoes, one fifteen-ounce can, not drained

- Coconut milk, unsweet, one cup

- Red pepper flakes, one quarter teaspoon

- Curry powder, two teaspoons

- Crunchy peanut butter, one tablespoon
- Lime juice, one tablespoon
- Rice, one cup cooked

Method:

Put the olive oil in a skillet over medium-high heat and fry the onion for five minutes. Add in the tomatoes, peanut butter, curry powder, coconut milk, and red pepper flakes and mix well. Set a lid on the skillet and let the mixture simmer for fifteen minutes. Stir the lime juice into the mix and serve it over the cooked rice.

Nutrition: Calories 414, 12 grams fiber, 61 grams carbs, 15 grams protein, 61 grams fat

4. BLACK BEAN CHILI

Prep fifteen min/cook twenty min/serves six

Ingredients:

- Canola oil, one tablespoon
- Red onion, one chopped
- Vegetable broth, three cups low salt
- Black beans, two fifteen-ounce cans
- Corn, whole kernel, two cans
- Crushed tomatoes, one can
- Vegan taco seasoning mix, three tablespoons

Method:

Heat the canola oil and stir in the onions. Fry them for three to four minutes until they feel soft. Stir in the taco seasoning and stir for one minute. Pour in the tomatoes, corn, broth, and beans and mix this all together well. Boil the chili and then let it simmer over a lower heat for ten minutes.

Calories 426, 16 grams fiber, 80 grams carbs, 19 grams protein, 5 grams fat

5. PESTO PASTA SALAD

Prep five min/cook ten min/serves two

Ingredients:

- Fusilli pasta, whole wheat, two cups
- Pesto, low fat, four tablespoons
- Spinach, one cup
- Salt, one half teaspoon
- Black pepper, one half teaspoon

Method:

Cook the fusilli, letting it get slightly overcooked so it will not be sticky when it is cold. Before draining the pasta, drop in the spinach and let it wilt for two to three minutes. Drain the water off the pasta and spinach and pour it into a bowl. Add the pesto, pepper, and salt and mix everything together well.

Nutrition: Calories 340, 10 grams protein, 4 grams fiber, 66 grams carbs, 2 grams fat

6. GREEN PEA FRITTER

Prep ten min/cook twenty min/makes ten

Ingredients:

- Frozen peas, two cups
- Olive oil, one tablespoon + one tablespoon

- Onion, one diced

- Garlic, three tablespoons

- Chickpea four, one and one half cups

- Baking soda, one teaspoon

- Salt, one quarter teaspoon

- Rosemary, one teaspoon

- Thyme, one half teaspoon

- Marjoram, one teaspoon

- Lemon juice, two tablespoons

Method:

Heat the oven to 350. Use spray oil to spray a baking sheet. Boil the peas for five minutes. Pour one tablespoon of olive oil in a skillet and fry the garlic and onion for five minutes. Pour the garlic and onion with the olive oil in a bowl and add the cooked peas, mashing them until they make a thick paste. Blend in the marjoram, thyme, rosemary, salt, baking soda, and chickpea flour. Dampen your hands and form the mash into ten equal-sized patties. Brush the patties with the other tablespoon of olive oil. Bake them for eighteen minutes in the oven, turning them over after nine minutes.

Nutrition one fritter: Calories 94, 4 grams protein, 3 grams fiber, 14 grams carbs, 3 grams fat

7. SPINACH POTATO CURRY

Prep fifteen min/cook forty-five min/serves four

Ingredients:

- Onion, one, chopped

- Garlic, minced, three tablespoon

- Ginger, ground, one teaspoon

- Green chili, one, chopped

- Olive oil, one tablespoon

- Cumin, ground, one teaspoon

- Coriander, ground, one teaspoon

- Tomatoes, three, diced

- Potatoes, three, cut into chunks

- Chickpeas, one fifteen ounce can, drain and rinse

- Spinach, two cups chopped

- Lemon juice, two tablespoons

- Water, two cups

- Rosemary, one teaspoon

Method:

In a large skillet or saucepan, put the olive oil and make it hot. Fry the garlic and onions for five minutes. Add in the diced tomatoes and the spices and mix well, then cook this for five minutes. Pour in the water, potatoes, and chickpeas and mix together well, and then cook the curry for thirty minutes. Drop in the chopped spinach and cook for five more minutes, stirring occasionally. Blend in the lemon juice and serve.

Nutrition: Calories 224, 9 grams protein, 7 grams fiber, 32 grams carbs, 5 grams fat

8. TOMATO, KALE, AND RICE SOUP

Prep ten min/cook twenty min/serves two

Ingredients:

- Olive oil, one tablespoon

- Garlic, minced, one tablespoon

- Ginger, ground, one teaspoon

- Kale, two cups chopped

- Cumin, ground, one half teaspoon

- Coriander, ground, one half teaspoon

- Tomatoes, two cans diced with juice

- Green bell pepper, diced

- Basmati rice, three tablespoons

Method:

Cook the bell pepper, garlic, and kale for five minutes in the olive oil. Stir in all of the spices and cook for one minute. Then pour in the tomatoes with the juice and the rice and stir well. Let the soup cook on low for twenty minutes to allow the rice to cook properly.

Nutrition: Calories 187, 5 grams protein, 2 grams fiber, 27 grams carbs, 6 grams fat

9. BLACK BEAN QUINOA CHILI

Prep fifteen min/cook thirty min/ serves four

Ingredients:

- Onion, one diced

- Garlic, minced, two tablespoons

- Cumin, ground, two teaspoons

- Paprika, one teaspoon

- Chili powder, one half teaspoon

- Quinoa, one cup rinsed well

- Vegetable broth, two cups

- Tomatoes, one chopped

- Black beans, one fifteen ounce can

- Avocado, one chopped
- Olive oil, one tablespoon

Method:

Fry the onion, garlic, and avocado in the olive oil for five minutes. Stir in the vegetable broth, tomatoes, quinoa, and the black beans. Mix this well and then let it simmer for thirty minutes or until the sauce is thick, and the quinoa is tender.

Nutrition: Calories 343, 15 grams protein, 13 grams fiber, 44 grams carbs, 9 grams fat

10. BLACK EYED PEAS WITH CHARD

Prep fifteen min/cook thirty min/serves six

Ingredients:

- Black-eyed peas, dried, one cup
- Salt, one-half teaspoon and one half teaspoon
- Olive oil, three tablespoons divided
- Onion, one medium-sized chopped fine
- Garlic, minced, two tablespoons
- Chard, one pound trimmed and chopped
- Vegetable broth, low salt, three cups
- Lemon juice, four tablespoons divided
- Water, four cups

Method:

Put the black-eyed peas in a bowl with one-half teaspoon of salt and cover them with cold water and let them sit overnight. Drain the water off and rinse them well. Put the peas in a pan with the four cups of water and the remaining half teaspoon of salt. Boil the water and then simmer the peas for fifteen minutes and drain them. Pour one tablespoon of olive oil in a skillet and cook the garlic and onion for five minutes, stirring occasionally. Add in the chard and cook for three to four minutes until the chard begins to wilt. Add in the broth, black-eyed peas, and two tablespoons of the lemon juice. Cook this on a simmer for twenty minutes. Pour in the last two tablespoons of lemon juice and olive oil, stir once, and serve.

Nutrition: Calories 186, 8 grams protein, 7 grams fiber, 23 grams carbs, 2 grams fat

11. WINTER GREENS WITH KUMQUATS AND POMEGRANATE

Prep thirty-five min/serves twelve

Ingredients:

- Pomegranate juice, six tablespoon
- Orange zest, one half teaspoon
- Orange juice, one and one half tablespoons
- Cornstarch, one and one half teaspoons
- Vegan Sugar, one and one half teaspoons
- Garlic powder, one half teaspoon
- Olive oil, one quarter cup
- Endives, two heads trimmed, separate the leaves
- Radicchio, one head, torn into pieces
- Arugula, five cups
- Pomegranate arils, one cup
- Kumquats, one-half cup thinly slices
- Walnuts, chopped, one quarter cup
- Pistachios, one-quarter cup chopped

Method:

Blend together the orange juice, cornstarch, sugar, orange zest, garlic powder, and pomegranate juice in a small pot and bring the mix to a boil. Let it boil for about five minutes, until it begins to darken, stirring often. Set the pot off to the side for twenty minutes to allow the mix to cool, then stir in the olive oil. While the sauce is cooling, arrange the arugula, radicchio, and endive on a large platter. Place the kumquats and pomegranate arils on top of the greens. Drizzle the sauce over the greens and top with the chopped pistachios and walnuts.

Nutrition per two cups: Calories 337, 30 grams protein, 6 grams fiber, 28 grams carbs, 13 grams fat

12. ROASTED MUSHROOMS AND SHALLOTS

Prep ten min/cook twenty min/serves four

Ingredients:

- Mushrooms, fresh, one pound cut into bite-size pieces
- Shallots, two cups sliced thick
- Olive oil, two tablespoons
- Thyme, dried, one teaspoon
- Salt, one quarter teaspoon
- Black pepper, one quarter teaspoon
- Red wine vinegar, one third cup

Method:

Heat your oven to 450. Place the shallots and mushrooms in a large bowl and add in the salt, pepper, thyme, and olive oil and toss the ingredients together to thoroughly coat the shallots and mushrooms. Roast the veggies on a baking sheet for fifteen minutes. Pour the red wine vinegar over the veggies and bake for five more minutes.

Nutrition: Calories 178, 5 grams protein, 4 grams fiber, 21 grams carbs, 7 grams fat

13. GARLIC CHILI ROASTED KOHLRABI

Prep twenty min/cook twenty min/serves six

Ingredients:

- Olive oil, two tablespoons
- Garlic, minced, one tablespoon
- Chili pepper, one teaspoon
- Salt, one quarter teaspoon
- Kohlrabi, one and one-half pounds, peel and cut into one half inch wedges
- Cilantro, fresh, chopped, two tablespoons

Method:

Heat your oven to 450. Mix together in a large bowl, the pepper, salt, chili pepper, garlic, and olive oil. Put in the kohlrabi and toss well to coat the kohlrabi. Bake the coated kohlrabi for twenty minutes, stirring it around when you are about halfway done with cooking. Sprinkle on the cilantro and serve.

Nutrition: Calories 76, 2 grams protein, 4 grams fiber, 7 grams carbs, 5 grams fat

14. LENTIL AND QUINOA CABBAGE ROLLS

Prep thirty min/cook two hours/serves four

Ingredients:

- Cabbage, one large head

Filling

- Lentils, three-fourths cup

- Water, three cups

- Quinoa, uncooked, one half cup

- Vegetable broth, one cup

- Onion, one diced

- Olive oil, one tablespoon

- Red wine vinegar, one tablespoon

- Soy sauce, two tablespoons

- Paprika, one teaspoon

Sauce

- Tomato puree, one twenty-eight ounce can

- Red wine vinegar, two teaspoons

- Salt, one half teaspoon

- Black pepper, one teaspoon

Method:

Put four inches of water into a pot and set the head of cabbage in the water. Boil the water and then cover the pot and turn down the heat. Let the cabbage head steam for twenty minutes and then set it to the side and let it cool slightly. While the cabbage is steaming, you can make the filling by first putting the water in a pot and adding the lentils. Boil the water and then let the lentils simmer for thirty minutes. They may need more water added as they cook. If any liquid is remaining after thirty minutes, drain the lentils. While the lentils are cooking, add the vegetable broth and quinoa to another pot. Let it boil and then simmer the quinoa for twenty minutes. Cover the pot and set the quinoa off to the side for five minutes, then fluff it with a fork. Put the oil in a skillet and fry the onion for three minutes. Mix in the lentils and the quinoa along with the seasonings. Stir this mix constantly for five minutes and then take the pan off the heat. Mix the sauce. Peel off one of the outer leaves from the head of cabbage and lay it on a work surface. Spoon on three or four tablespoons of the lentil quinoa mix and then roll the leaf up and lay it in a thirteen by nine-inch baking dish. Keep filling cabbage leaves until all of the mix is used. Cover the cabbage rolls with the sauce. Then cover the dish and bake the rolls for one hour.

Nutrition: Calories 394, 19 grams protein, 22 grams fiber, 5 grams carbs, 6 grams fat

15. CHARD, LENTIL, AND POTATO SLOW COOKER SOUP

Prep twenty min/cook eight hours/serves six

Ingredients:

- Olive oil, one tablespoon
- Onion, one large diced
- Celery, one stalk sliced
- Carrot, one sliced
- Garlic, minced, two tablespoons
- Swiss chard, one bunch, torn into small pieces
- Lentils, one cup rinsed
- Potatoes, four medium-sized, peeled and cut into chunks
- Vegetable broth, six cups
- Tamari, one tablespoon
- Salt, one half teaspoon
- Black pepper, one teaspoon

Method:

Fry the carrot, garlic, onion, and celery in the olive oil for five minutes, stirring often, for ten minutes. Put the cooked veggies into a slow cooker along with the soy sauce, broth, potatoes, and lentils. Stir once or twice and then cover the slow cooker and cook the soup on low heat for seven and one-half hours. Then stir in the salt, pepper, and chard leaves and cook for thirty more minutes.

Nutrition: Calories 176, 10 grams protein, 27 grams carbs, 10 grams fiber, 5 grams fat

1. TOFU SCRAMBLE WITH SPINACH

Prep five min/cook ten min/serves two

Ingredients:

- Olive oil, two tablespoons
- Tomatoes, two chopped fine
- Garlic, minced, two tablespoons
- Mushrooms, fresh, three-fourths cup
- Spinach, one large bunch
- Tofu, one pound extra firm well pressed and crumbled
- Soy sauce, one half teaspoon
- Lemon juice, one teaspoon
- Salt, one half teaspoon
- Black pepper, one teaspoon

Method:

Fry the mushrooms, garlic, and tomatoes in the olive oil for three to four minutes. Mix in the soy sauce, lemon juice, tofu crumbles, and spinach, stirring the ingredients to mix them well. Cook this for seven to eight minutes. Add in the salt and pepper, stir once, and serve.

Nutrition: Calories 527, 36 grams protein, 43 grams carbs, 29 grams fat, 10 grams fiber

2. TABBOULEH SALAD WITH EDAMAME

Prep thirty-five min/serves four

Ingredients:

- Bulgur wheat, one and one-fourth cups uncooked
- Water, two cups boiling
- Pesto, one quarter cup
- Lemon juice, three tablespoons
- Cherry tomatoes, two cups chopped
- Nutritional yeast, one half cup
- Chickpeas, one fifteen ounce can drain and rinse
- Scallions, one-third cup sliced
- Parsley, dried, two tablespoons
- Black pepper, one half teaspoon
- Edamame, shelled, two cups

Method:

Pour the uncooked bulgur into a large bowl and pour the boiling water over it. Cover the bowl with a plate and let the bulgur stand for thirty minutes, and then drain it. Mix the lemon juice and the pesto together. Then put the pesto into the bulgur and add in the pepper, parsley, edamame, green onions, chickpeas, and tomatoes. Toss all the ingredients gently but completely. Sprinkle the nutritional yeast over the mixture and serve.

Nutrition: Calories 570, 23 grams protein 93 grams carbs, 16 grams fat, 14 grams fiber

3. KOREAN TOFU BOWL

Prep fifteen min/cook ten min/serves two

Ingredients:

- Tofu, firm, pressed and drained, baked, one cup
- Sesame oil, two tablespoons
- Broccoli, cooked, one cup
- Tamari, low carb, one tablespoon
- Cauliflower rice, two cups
- Sesame seeds, two teaspoons
- Mushrooms, cooked, one half of one cup
- Scallions, chopped, one half cup

Method:

In a large skillet fry the cauliflower rice, baked tofu, cooked broccoli, and cooked mushrooms in the sesame oil for fifteen minutes. Then stir in the sesame seeds and the tamari and mix them in well. Place the mixture into two bowls and top each bowl with the chopped scallions.

Nutrition: Calories 247, 18 grams protein, 13 grams fat, 5 grams fiber, 9 grams carbs

4. ZUCCHINI RAVIOLI

Prep twenty-five min/cook thirty-five min/serves six

Ingredients:

Topping

- Marinara sauce, one large jar any vegan flavor

Pine Nut Hemp Parmesan

- Pine nuts, one-quarter of one cup

- Salt, one quarter teaspoon

- Hemp seeds, one-quarter of one cup

Zucchini

- Basil, fresh, one cup

- Zucchini, four medium-sized

- Black pepper, one half teaspoon

- Water, one cup

- Cashews, raw, one cup

- Walnuts, one cup

- Garlic, minced, three tablespoons

- Spinach, fresh, one cup

- Salt, one half teaspoon

Method:

Heat the oven to 350. Mash the hemp seeds and the pine nuts and mix the salt in, and then set this bowl to the side. Wipe off the zucchini and peel it, then slice it into thin slices lengthwise. Each zucchini should make between twelve and fifteen slices. Place the slices of zucchini on a plate covered with paper towels and lightly salt them. Leave them laying there while you blend together the cashews, garlic, walnuts, pepper, salt, basil, spinach, and water. You will want to chop the nuts and greens until they are in very small pieces. Now use a paper towel to wipe off the water on the zucchini that was drawn out by the salt. Lay two slices of zucchini on a plate in the shape of an 'X.' Put a spoon of the mix in the middle and bring the end of the strips to the middle to make a pocket. Continue making pockets with the zucchini strips and the mix and placing them in a thirteen by nine-inch baking dish. When you have made all of the pockets, cover them with the pine nut parmesan. Bake the dish for forty minutes and let it sit for five minutes before you serve. One serving is five ravioli.

Nutrition: Calories 360, 12 grams protein, 15 grams carbs, 30 grams fat, 12 grams fiber

5. SUSHI BOWL

Prep five min/serves one

Ingredients:

Toppings

- Sesame seeds, one teaspoon
- Avocado, one-quarter of one sliced
- Parsley, one tablespoon

Bowl

- Tofu, firm, pressed, four ounces
- Cauliflower rice, cooked, one half of one cup
- Salad greens, one cup packed
- Cucumber, one-quarter of one cup cubed

Method:

Put the tofu in a bowl with the cucumber, salad greens, and the cooked cauliflower rice and mix these together gently but completely. Use another bowl to mix together the parsley, sesame seeds, and avocado for the topping. Put the topping mix on top of the bowl mix and enjoy it.

Nutrition: Calories 289, 16 grams protein, 6 grams carbs, 9 grams fiber, 21 grams fat

6. MINI BLACK BEAN PITAS

Prep one hour/cook thirty min/serves eight

Ingredients:

Sauce

- Mini pita breads, sixteen

- Tomatoes, two chopped
- Red onion, one half thin sliced
- Dill, fresh, two tablespoons chopped
- Black pepper, one teaspoon
- Garlic, minced, one tablespoon
- Romaine lettuce, four leaves shred
- Parsley, fresh, one quarter cup chop
- Lemon juice, one tablespoon
- Salt, one half teaspoon
- Cucumber, one half thin sliced

Black Beans

- Olive oil, one quarter cup
- Black beans, canned drained and rinsed, two cups
- Paprika, one quarter teaspoon
- Black pepper, one teaspoon
- Garlic powder, two teaspoons
- Lemon juice, two tablespoons
- Cumin, ground, one teaspoon
- Lemon zest, one tablespoon
- Coriander, ground, three quarters teaspoon

Method:

Drain the liquid off the black beans and place them in a mixing bowl with the olive oil, garlic powder, paprika, lemon zest, lemon juice, pepper, cumin, coriander and mix well. Set this bowl in the refrigerator for one hour to let the flavors blend well together. While it is blending, mix the garlic, salt, pepper, parsley, and the dill. Bring out the bean mix and pour it into a skillet and let it boil. Pour in the ingredients of the other bowl and mix well. Let the mix simmer until most of the liquid is cooked off, then fill the pitas.

Nutrition: Calories 154, 12 grams protein, 5 grams fiber, 10 grams carbs, 16 grams fat

7. TOMATOES AND TOFU

Prep five min/cook twenty min/serves two

Ingredients:

- Tofu, one block medium, unpressed, cut into rounds one-half-inch thick
- Black pepper, one teaspoon
- Tomatoes, one fifteen ounce can diced
- Chili powder, one quarter teaspoon
- Thyme, one quarter teaspoon
- Garlic, minced, two tablespoons
- Salt, one teaspoon
- Olive oil, one tablespoon
- Rosemary, one teaspoon
- Oregano, one teaspoon

Method:

Fry the minced garlic in the olive oil for two minutes, and then blend in the tomatoes with the salt, pepper, chili powder, oregano, thyme, and rosemary. Stir these together well and then let this simmer for five minutes. Then lay the slices of tofu on top of this mix in the skillet and let it simmer without stirring for fifteen minutes.

Nutrition: Calories 284, 20 grams protein, 5 grams fiber, 16 grams carbs, 10 grams fat

8. THAI SOUP

Prep ten min/cook fifteen min/serves four

Ingredients:

- Mushrooms, three sliced thinly
- Bell pepper, red, one-half cut in julienne strips
- Vegetable broth, two cups
- Cilantro, one half of one cup chopped
- Tofu, firm, pressed and cubed, ten ounces
- Coconut milk, one fourteen ounce can
- Thai chili, finely chopped, one half of one
- Garlic, minced, two tablespoons
- Tamari, one tablespoon
- Ginger, ground, one tablespoon
- Onion, red, one-half cut in julienne strips
- Lime juice, two tablespoons

Method:

Blend the coconut milk and the vegetable broth together in a large pot. Add the garlic, ground ginger, and mushrooms, onion, red bell pepper, and Thai chili. Boil this for five minutes while you stir it frequently. Drop in the tofu and cook the soup for five more minutes. Blend in the tamari, lime juice, and cilantro and remove the pot from the stove.

Nutrition: Calories 339, 15 grams protein, 6 grams fiber, 27 grams fat, 8 grams carbs

9. NIÇOISE SALAD

Prep forty min/serves four

Ingredients:

Dressing

- Olive oil, three tablespoons

- Black pepper, one half teaspoon

- Water, one tablespoon

- Garlic, minced, one tablespoon

- Salt, one quarter teaspoon

- Lemon juice, two tablespoons

Salad

- Tofu, extra firm, eight ounces crumbled into small pieces

- Basil leaves, chopped fine, one half of one cup

- Salt, one half teaspoon

- Bibb lettuce, one large head

- Red onion, thin-sliced, one half of one cup

- Black olives, pitted, one half of one cup

- Olive oil, one tablespoon

- Black pepper, one teaspoon

- Green beans, French style, four ounces

- Grape tomatoes, one cup

Method:

Boil the green beans for five minutes over high heat. Make the dressing by first blending together the water with the lemon juice and oil. Then blend in all of the spices and set this bowl off to the side. Set the dressing in the refrigerator and take the beans off the stove and drain off the liquid. Set out four serving plates and lay of the leaves of Bibb lettuce. On the lettuce lay the black olives, onions, tofu, green beans, and tomatoes in even amounts, piling them all together in the center or arranging them attractively, your choice. Serve the salads with the cold dressing on the side for topping.

Nutrition: Calories 350, 22 grams protein, 11 grams fat, 10 grams fiber, 12 grams carbs

10. SPICED LENTIL SOUP

Prep twenty min/cook one hour/serves eight

Ingredients:

- Yellow onion, one chopped fine
- Black pepper, one teaspoon
- Vegetable broth, seven cups
- Celery, fine chop, one half of one cup
- Tomato, two larges, cleaned and diced
- Cilantro, chopped, one half of one cup
- Salt, one half teaspoon
- Cinnamon, one tablespoon
- Ginger, two tablespoons minced
- Parsley, fresh, chopped, one half of one cup
- Lentils, dry, one half of one cup
- Paprika, one tablespoon
- Olive oil, three tablespoons

Method:

Fry the celery, onion, garlic, and ginger in the olive oil for ten minutes, stirring frequently. Blend in the cinnamon, salt, turmeric, pepper, and paprika and let this cook for five more minutes. Now add in the cilantro, lentils, tomatoes, and broth and mix well. Let this soup simmer for thirty minutes.

Nutrition: Calories 240, 14 grams protein, 8 grams fiber, 8 grams fat, 15 grams carbs

11. MUSHROOMS WITH GREENS

Prep forty min/cook fifty-five min/serves four

Ingredients:

- Portobello mushroom caps, four large with gills removed
- Lemon juice, one teaspoon
- Arugula or spinach, two cups, cleaned and chopped and cooked as desired
- Tomato, one large sliced into four slices
- Black pepper, one half teaspoon
- Olive oil, one tablespoon
- Coconut cream, one-quarter of one cup
- Eggplant, four slices
- Salt, one half teaspoon
- Garlic, minced, one tablespoon

Method:

Cream together the garlic, lemon juice, and the coconut cream. Use the olive oil to coat the mushroom caps and slices of eggplant and then fry them for ten minutes, five on each side. Set out four serving plates and lay one mushroom cap, inside facing up, on each plate. Then divide the coconut mixture among the four caps. Top the coconut mixture with a slice of cooked eggplant. Then divide the cooked greens among the four stacks and top each stack with a slice of tomato. If any of the coconut cream mix is leftover, then you can use it to drizzle over the stacks for decoration.

Nutrition: Calories 289, 10 grams protein, 7 grams fiber, 11 grams fat, 15 grams carbs

12. MEDITERRANEAN STYLE BURRITO

Prep fifteen min/cook five min/serves six

Ingredients:

- Tortillas, ten-inch size, whole wheat, six
- Avocado oil, two tablespoons
- Tomatoes, chopped, three tablespoons
- Refried beans, vegan, canned, three-fourths of one cup
- Black olives, sliced, three tablespoons
- Nutritional yeast, one half of one cup
- Spinach, two cups, washed and dried
- Salsa for garnish

Method:

Fry the tomatoes, black olives, and spinach in the avocado oil for five minutes, stirring frequently. Lay out the six tortillas and divide the refried bean mix among the six tortillas, then spread it out thinly but do not go all the way to the edge. Cover the beans with equal portions of the veggie mix. Fold the sides of each tortilla in and then roll up the tortillas. Lay the rolled tortillas in the skillet where you cooked the veggies and fry them for three minutes on each side. Top the burritos with the salsa and serve.

Nutrition: Calories 252, 14 grams protein, 6 grams fiber, 11 grams fat, 19 grams carbs

13. GREEK SALAD

Prep fifteen min/serves six

Ingredients:

Dressing

- Salt, one quarter teaspoon
- Balsamic vinegar, two tablespoons

- Oregano, one quarter teaspoon

- Black pepper, one half teaspoon

- Olive oil, one-third of one cup

- Garlic, minced, one tablespoon

Salad

- Yellow bell pepper, cleaned and diced

- Black olives, one half of one cup slice

- Salt, one quarter teaspoon

- Cherry tomatoes, one cup slice

- Romaine lettuce, four cups chop

- Cucumber, one peeled, quarter and slice

- Nutritional yeast, one half of one cup

- Olive oil, two tablespoons

- Red onion, one small thin-slice

- Parsley, fresh, one half of one cup chop

Method:

Blend all of the spices for the dressing into the olive oil; this is best done in some sort of shaker bottle. Set this off to the side. Toss together in a large bowl, the olives, bell pepper, cucumber, onion, tomatoes, and parsley, mixing them together gently but well. Set out six serving bowls and divide the salad mix evenly among the bowls. Drizzle a bit of the dressing onto each bowl and then top them with the nutritional yeast.

Nutrition: Calories 294, 15 grams protein, 12 grams fat, 11 grams fiber, 11 grams carbs

14. SPICY SPAGHETTI SQUASH

Prep forty min/cook thirty min/serves two

Ingredients:

- Thyme, dried, one half teaspoon
- Avocado oil, two tablespoons
- Spinach, fresh or frozen chopped finely, one cup
- Cherry tomatoes, eight with each cut in three slices
- Spaghetti squash, one large
- Chickpeas, one-third of one cup, drained and rinsed
- Salt, one half teaspoon
- Garlic, minced, one tablespoon
- Chili powder, one half teaspoon
- Marjoram, dried, one teaspoon
- Cumin, one teaspoon
- Rosemary, dried, one teaspoon
- Nutritional yeast, two tablespoons
- Onion, red, one-quarter of one cup sliced thinly

Method:

Heat the oven to 400. Wash off and dry the spaghetti squash and then cut it in half the long way. Scoop out the seeds and discard them. Use one tablespoon of the avocado oil to brush over the inside of the squash. Place the halves of squash on a baking sheet, inside facing down, and poke several holes in the skin with a knife point or a fork to allow the steam to escape. Bake the squash halves for thirty minutes. Scrape out the squash using a fork so that it will resemble strands of spaghetti. Put this into a bowl and throw away the squash shells. Set the spaghetti off to the side. With the leftover avocado oil fry the garlic and onion for five minutes while you stir constantly. Then add in the marjoram, cumin, rosemary, tomatoes, chili powder, chickpeas, and thyme until well blended and cook this for five more minutes. Blend in the spaghettis squash to this mix with the spinach and salt and stir constantly while this cooks for five minutes more. Top each serving with the nutritional yeast.

Nutrition: Calories 272, 11 grams protein, 5 grams fiber, 14 grams carbs, 10 grams fat

15. CAULIFLOWER PIE

Prep thirty min/cook thirty min/serves four

Ingredients:

- Vegetable broth, one cup
- Balsamic vinegar, one-quarter of one cup
- Tomato paste, one tablespoon
- Black pepper, one teaspoon
- Nutritional yeast, three tablespoons
- Thyme, dried, one teaspoon
- Carrots, two medium-sized peeled and diced fine
- Salt, one half teaspoon
- Cauliflower, one head
- Nutmeg, ground, one teaspoon
- Onion, one medium-sized diced finely
- Celery, one stalk washed and diced fine
- Olive oil, two tablespoons
- Dijon mustard, one tablespoon
- Olive oil, two tablespoons + two tablespoons
- Garlic, minced, three tablespoons
- Mushrooms, diced small, one cup

Method:

Heat the oven to 400. Chop the cauliflower into bite-size pieces and cook it in boiling water for ten minutes. Drain off the water and place the cooked cauliflower into a bowl and set it to the side. Then fry the carrots, onion, and celery in two tablespoons of the olive oil in a large skillet, stirring occasionally for five minutes. Drop in the mushrooms and cook for five minutes more. Now add the tomato paste and balsamic vinegar and mix for two minutes, and then pour in the vegetable broth. Simmer all of this for ten minutes or until about half of the liquid has been absorbed by the foods. Mash the cauliflower in the bowl while you are waiting for this to cook. Blend into the mashed cauliflower the nutmeg, thyme, salt, mustard, and nutritional yeast with the other two tablespoons of the avocado oil. Spoon the veggie mix into a nine by nine-inch baking dish and top it with the mashed cauliflower mixture. Bake this for twenty minutes.

Nutrition: Calories 400, 11 grams protein, 9 grams fiber, 15 grams carbs, 15 grams fat

RECIPES FOR RECOVERY

After a good workout, a good recovery meal is important. Your cortisol levels will be high while your blood sugar will be low. This is when you will need a good mix of carbs and protein. You will be hungry after a workout, and it is important to eat good, healthy food and not grab something that is full of refined carbs. You will also want foods that are rich in omega-3 acids and antioxidants to help remove the inflammation in your muscles from the workout. You will want to eat foods low in fat because dietary fat will slow your digestion and prevent the food from getting where it needs to be, like your muscles.

1. CUCUMBER TOMATO TOAST

Prep five min/serves one

Ingredients:

- Olive oil, one teaspoon
- Vegan cream cheese, two teaspoons softened
- Oregano, dried, one quarter teaspoon
- Tomato, one half diced
- Whole grain flatbread, two slices
- Salt, one quarter teaspoon
- Balsamic vinegar, one teaspoon
- Black pepper, one half teaspoon
- Cucumber, one half diced

Method:

Blend together the diced tomato, olive oil, oregano, salt, and pepper. Spread the softened cream cheese onto the flatbread and top the slices with the tomato mixture. Drizzle the bread with the balsamic vinegar.

Nutrition: Calories 177, 3 grams fiber, 3 grams protein, 8 grams fat, 24 grams carbs

2. AVOCADO TOAST

Prep five min/serves one

Ingredients:

- Salt, one quarter teaspoon
- Black pepper, one half teaspoon
- Avocado, one peeled and sliced thinly
- Whole grain bread, two slices toasted

Method:

Slice the avocado while the bread is toasting. Lay the slices of avocado onto the toast and sprinkle on the pepper and salt.

Nutrition: Calories 362, 10 grams protein, ten grams fiber, 30 grams carbs, 25 grams fat

3. ORANGE BANANA SMOOTHIE

Prep five min/serves two

Ingredients:

- Ice cubes if desired
- Kale, two cups

- Almond milk, one cup

- Pear, fresh, one cored

- Banana, one

- Grapes, red or green, one cup

- Orange, one peeled

Method:

Chop all of the ingredients into small bits and then blend them in a blender for two minutes. You can use some ice cubes if you want to make it colder.

Nutrition: Calories 110, 4 grams fiber, 3 grams protein, 24 grams carbs, 2 grams fat

4. SPINACH STRAWBERRY SALAD

Prep ten min/serves four

Ingredients:

- Baby spinach, six cups

- Apple, any color, one cored and diced

- Onion, one diced

- Pomegranate seeds, one half cup

- Strawberries, sliced, one cup

- Pecans, one-quarter cup chopped

- Yogurt, soy one quarter cup

- Apple cider vinegar, two tablespoons

- Raspberry jam, all fruit, one quarter cup

- Dijon mustard, two teaspoons

- Salt, one eighth teaspoon

Method:

Mix together in a large bowl the pomegranate seeds, strawberries, pecans, onion, apple, and baby spinach. In a different smaller bowl or a shaker, jar mix together the apple cider vinegar, Dijon mustard, raspberry jam, salt, and yogurt together. Pour all of the dressing over the salad and toss it all gently but well.

Nutrition: Calories 168, 5 grams fiber, 28 grams carbs, 6 grams fat, 4 grams protein

5. ENERGY RECOVERY BARS

Prep: five min / Servings: 4

Ingredients:

- Chia seeds, one tablespoon
- Dehydrated Cranberries, one cup
- Almonds, one cup
- Dates, one cup
- Flax seeds, one tablespoon
- Agave, two tablespoons

Method:

You will want to start this recipe by taking out a food processor and placing the almonds and dates in. Go ahead and pulse the ingredients together before adding in the rest of them.

Now that you have your mixture take a baking dish and line it with parchment paper. When you are ready, pour the mixture into the baking dish and push it down with your fingers. When this is all set, place the dish into the fridge and allow to harden for two hours before you cut it into bars.

Nutrition: Calories 410, 50 grams carbs, 20 grams fats, 10 grams proteins

6. BEET AND BERRY SMOOTHIE

Prep five min/serves two

Ingredients:

- Frozen mixed berries, one and one half cups
- Banana, one broken into pieces
- Almond milk, unsweetened, one and one half cups
- Beet, one raw peeled and chunked
- Beet greens, one bunch, washed and chopped
- Orange juice, one quarter cup

Method:

Place all of the ingredients into a blender and start blending, first on low to mix all of the ingredients together and then gradually increasing the speed to break down and smooth all of the ingredients.

Nutrition: Calories 88, 4 grams fiber, 2 grams protein, 18 grams carbs, 2 grams fat

7. TOFU BELL PEPPER STIR FRY

Prep twenty min/serves four

Ingredients:

- Olive oil, one-fourth cup divided
- Cornstarch, five tablespoons divided
- Tofu, extra firm, one fourteen ounce pack drained and cubed
- Orange juice, one half cup
- Onion, one cup thinly sliced

- Green bell pepper, one sliced thinly

- Garlic, minced, one tablespoon

- Orange zest, one teaspoon

- Crushed red pepper, one half teaspoon

- Soy sauce, three tablespoons

- Rice vinegar, one tablespoon

- Vegan sugar, one teaspoon

- Salt, one half teaspoon

- Brown rice, two cups precooked

- Cilantro, chopped, two tablespoons

Method:

Mix the tofu with one-quarter cup of the cornstarch in a bowl and toss them together well. Fry the tofu for eight minutes in three tablespoons of the olive oil, then remove the tofu from the pan and set it to the side. Blend the leftover cornstarch with the orange juice. Add the leftover oil to the pan and cook the bell peppers and onions for five minutes. Mix in the crushed red pepper, orange zest, and garlic and mix well. Stir in the salt, sugar, vinegar, soy sauce, and juice mix and bring to a boil. Stir in the tofu well and take off the stove. Put a one-half cup of rice on each plate and top it with three-fourths cup of the tofu mix and garnish with cilantro.

Nutrition: Calories 488, 6 grams fiber, 17 grams protein, 12 grams fat, 59 grams carbs

8. PEACH GRAPEFRUIT GINGER SMOOTHIE

Prep five min/serves two

Ingredients:

- Banana, frozen, one half

- Mint, fresh, chopped, one teaspoon

- Peaches, frozen, one cup
- Ginger, ground, one teaspoon
- Grapefruit juice, one cup

Method:

Blend well in the blender, slowly at first, and then increasing the speed to break down the fruit and blend it well.

Nutrition: Calories 187, 4 grams fiber, 2 grams fat, 13 grams protein, 32 grams carbs

9. SESAME AVOCADO HUMMUS DIP

Prep ten min/serves one

Make this before your workout, so it is ready for you afterward.

Ingredients:

- Chickpeas, one fifteen ounce can
- Avocado, one
- Tahini, one quarter cup
- Water, three tablespoons
- Sesame oil, two tablespoons
- Rice vinegar, one tablespoon
- Salt, one half teaspoon
- Garlic, minced, one tablespoon
- Green onions, two tablespoons diced
- Celery, two stalks cleaned and slices
- Baby carrots, one quarter cup
- Red bell pepper, one half sliced

Method:

After draining and rinsing the chickpeas and put them into a mixing bowl with the tahini, avocado, sesame oil, salt, garlic, water, and rice vinegar. Mash the avocado and the chickpeas while you are mixing these ingredients together well. Scoop the hummus into a bowl and top it with the green onions. Serve the hummus with the prepared bell pepper, carrots, and celery.

Nutrition: Calories 126, 2 grams fiber, 10 grams carbs, 4 grams protein, 8 grams fat

10. POTATO SALAD WITH MUSTARD SAUCE

Prep ten min/cook twenty min/serves four

Another great dish to make in advance!

Ingredients:

- Olive oil, one quarter cup
- Balsamic vinegar, three tablespoons
- Mustard, two tablespoons
- Black pepper, one half teaspoon
- Salt, one quarter teaspoon
- Russet potatoes, two washed and cut into chunks
- Onion, one half cut into thin slices
- Chives, fresh, chopped, two tablespoons

Method:

Put the potato chunks into a pot of water and boil them for twenty minutes. While they are boiling, mix together the salt, pepper, mustard, balsamic vinegar, and olive oil. After the potatoes have cooked, drain them well and add them to the bowl with the dressing mix, then toss all of the ingredients to mix them well. Stir in the onion and the chives. This recipe can be consumed cold or hot.

Nutrition: Calories 231, 4 grams fiber, 26 grams carbs, 2 grams protein, 13 grams fat

11. ROAST CHILI LIME CHICKPEAS

Prep five min/cook thirty min/serves two

Ingredients:

- Chickpeas, one fifteen ounce can drained and rinsed
- Olive oil, two tablespoons
- Chili powder, two teaspoons
- Lime zest, two tablespoons
- Salt, one half teaspoon

Method:

Heat the oven to 400. Dry the drained chickpeas by patting them with a paper towel. Place the chickpeas into a bowl with the olive oil and toss them together well. Bake the chickpeas for thirty minutes on a baking sheet. After they have baked, place them back into the bowl and toss with the salt, lime zest, and chili powder.

Nutrition: Calories 151, 4 grams fiber, 19 grams carbs, 6 grams protein, 6 grams fat

12. VEGGIE PINTO BEANS

Prep ten min/cook fifteen min/serves four

Ingredients:

- Pinto beans, one fifteen ounce can rinsed and drained

- Salt, one half teaspoon

- Apple cider vinegar, one tablespoon

- Tomato paste, two tablespoons

- Water, one half cup

- Red bell pepper, one cup chopped fine

- Yellow onion, one cup chopped fine

- Olive oil, one tablespoon

Method:

Fry the pepper and onion for five minutes in the olive oil. Blend in the vinegar, salt, tomato paste, and water. Cook for ten minutes and then stir in the beans and cook for three minutes more.

Nutrition: Calories 147, 7 grams fiber, 6 grams protein, 22 grams carbs, 4 grams fat

13. PUMPKIN SPICE OVERNIGHT OATS

Prep ten min/sets overnight/serves one

If you prefer to workout first thing in the morning, then this will be ready for you to grab and take it with you.

Ingredients:

- Pumpkin puree, one half cup

- Cinnamon, one teaspoon

- Cloves, one half teaspoon

- Nutmeg, one half teaspoon

- Old fashioned oats, one cup

- Almond milk, one cup

Method:

In a jar that has a lid that will attach snugly, put all of the ingredients together. In the morning before eating, just stir the oats well.

Nutrition: Calories 250, 9 grams protein, 5 grams fat, 4 grams fiber, 33 grams carbs

14. GREEN SMOOTHIE BOWL

Prep fifteen min/serves two

Ingredients:

- Banana, one medium sliced
- Frozen spinach, two cups chopped
- Pineapple cubes, one half cup
- Water as needed
- Kiwi, two small peeled and chopped
- Hempseed, two tablespoons
- Salt, one eighth teaspoon
- Ginger, ground, two teaspoons
- Raspberries, fresh, one half cup
- Blueberries, fresh, one half cup
- Shredded coconut, unsweetened, one half cup

Method:

Place the banana, hempseed, salt, ginger, kiwis, spinach, and pineapple into the blender and begin blending, slowly at first to break up the food, then increasing the speed until the ingredients are all creamy and smooth. Pour the creamy smoothie into two bowls and top with the blueberries, raspberries, and coconut.

Nutrition: Calories 230, 9 grams protein, 7 grams fiber, 5 grams fat, 38 grams carbs

15. STRAWBERRY COCONUT GRANOLA

Prep five min/cook twenty-five min/makes ten one-half cup servings

Ingredients:

- Rolled oats, one and one half cups
- Almonds, roughly chopped, one and three-fourths cup
- Vegan sugar, two tablespoons
- Salt, one eighth teaspoon
- Coconut oil, melted, three and one half tablespoons
- Maple syrup, one quarter cup
- Coconut flakes, unsweetened, one half cup
- Strawberries, frozen or fresh, one cup

Method:

Heat the oven to 340. Put the sugar, salt, nuts, and oats in a mixing bowl and combine well. Place the maple syrup and the coconut oil in a pot on the stove and warm for three minutes while you are mixing well together. Pour this immediately over the dry ingredients and stir them well to coat all pieces. Place all of this on to a large baking sheet in a single layer and bake for twenty minutes. Then add in the coconut and stir the granola around and bake for eight more minutes. When the granola has cooled completely add in the strawberries.

Nutrition: Calories 248, 6 grams protein, 4 grams fiber, 20 grams carbs, 17 grams fat

1. GRILLED EGGPLANT ROLLS

Prep five min/cook eight min/serves eight

Ingredients:

- Olive oil, two tablespoons

- Eggplant, one medium

- Basil, fresh, chopped, two tablespoons

- Tomato, one large

- Onion, one half sliced paper-thin

- Bell pepper, one half sliced paper-thin

Method:

Slice the peeled eggplant into slices lengthwise that are about a quarter-inch thick and throw away the ends. Slice the bell pepper, tomato, and onion very thinly and set them off to the side. Brush all of the slices of eggplant with olive oil and fry them in a hot skillet for three minutes on each side. Then lay the slices of eggplant onto a work surface, lay one slice each of the veggies on one end, season with the basil and pepper, and then roll the eggplant strips up and serve.

Nutrition: Calories 59, 3 grams fat, 6 grams fiber, 4 grams carbs, 3 grams protein

2. CAULIFLOWER FRIED RICE

Prep five min/cook ten min/serves four

Ingredients:

- Riced cauliflower, twelve ounces frozen or fresh
- Green onion, one quarter cup
- Sesame oil, one tablespoon
- Garlic, minced, two tablespoons
- Soy sauce, two tablespoons
- Tofu, firm, cut into crumbles
- Carrot, one-quarter cup chopped fine

Method:

Fry the riced cauliflower and the carrots in the sesame oil for five minutes while stirring occasionally. Add in the green onion and the garlic and cook one more minute. Stir in the tofu crumbles and cook for three minutes, then stir in the soy sauce and serve.

Nutrition: Calories 114, 4 grams fiber, 8 grams fat, 4 grams protein, 6 grams carbs

3. SPIRAL ZUCCHINI WITH GRAPE TOMATOES

Prep five min/cook ten min/serves two

Ingredients:

- Zucchini, one large cut in spirals
- Olive oil, one tablespoon
- Basil, fresh, chopped, one tablespoon
- Garlic, minced, two tablespoons

- Black pepper, one teaspoon

- Grape tomatoes, one cup cut in half

- Rosemary, one teaspoon

- Onion, chopped, one half cup

- Salt, one half teaspoon

- Crushed red pepper flakes, one quarter teaspoon

- Lemon juice, one tablespoon

Method:

Fry the minced garlic and the onion in the olive oil for five minutes. Mix in the red pepper flakes, pepper, salt, and tomatoes and blend well, then lower the heat and simmer for fifteen minutes. Then stir in the zucchini noodles with the rosemary and basil. Increase the heat and cook for three minutes, then drizzle the mix with the lemon juice and serve.

Nutrition: Calories 117, 7 grams fiber, 13 grams carbs, 5 grams fat, 4 grams protein

4. SWEET POTATO SQUASH PATTIES

Prep fifteen min/cook ten min/serves two

Ingredients:

- Cumin, ground, one quarter teaspoon

- Olive oil, two tablespoons

- Squash, shredded, one cup

- Salt, one half teaspoon

- Sweet potato, cooked and mashed, two cups

- Black pepper, one teaspoon

- Garlic powder, one half teaspoon

- Parsley, dried, one quarter teaspoon

Method:

Stir together in a mixing bowl, the squash, and sweet potato. Put in all of the spices and mix all the ingredients well together. Divide the mix into four equal size portions and fry the patties in the olive oil for five minutes on each side in a large skillet.

Nutrition one patty: Calories 112, 5 grams fiber, 9 grams fat, 3 grams protein, 6 grams carbs

5. CORN AND OKRA CASSEROLE

Prep twenty min/cook thirty min/serves six

Ingredients:

- Onion, one small, sliced
- Okra, one pound
- Corn, whole kernel, one can
- Garlic, one clove sliced
- Green bell pepper, one cleaned and sliced
- Parsley, chopped, one tablespoon
- Tomatoes, two large diced
- Olive oil, three tablespoons

Method:

Heat the oven to 375. Chop the okra into small chunks. Fry the green pepper, okra, onion, and garlic in the olive oil for ten minutes, stirring often. Add in the tomatoes and parsley and cook for ten minutes more. Blend in the corn and then pour the mix into a nine by nine-inch baking dish and bake uncovered for thirty minutes.

Nutrition: Calories 125, 8 grams fiber, 2 grams fat, 4 grams protein, 17 grams carbs

6. FUSILLI WITH SQUASH AND TOMATO

Prep twenty-five min/serves six

Ingredients:

- Fusilli pasta, twelve ounces, cooked
- Olive oil, two tablespoons
- Grape tomatoes, two cups, sliced in half
- Black pepper, one half teaspoon
- Thyme, chop, one tablespoon
- Rosemary, one half teaspoon
- Squash, yellow, one pound
- Salt, one half teaspoon
- Onion, yellow, one thin slice

Method:

Peel the squash and cut off the neck, then cut it into chunks. Fry the squash, pepper, onion, salt, and thyme in the olive oil for ten minutes. Pour in the tomatoes and cook for five minutes more. Add in the cooked pasta and stir together well and serve.

Nutrition: Calories 311, 10 grams protein, 4 grams fiber, 49 grams carbs, 9 grams fat

7. LIMA BEAN CASSEROLE

Prep fifteen min/cook thirty min/serves five

Ingredients:

- Cumin, one teaspoon
- Lima beans, canned two cups

- Salt, one half teaspoon
- Lemon juice, two teaspoons
- Dry mustard, two teaspoons
- Thyme, one half teaspoon
- Olive oil, two tablespoons
- Black pepper, one teaspoon
- Nutritional yeast, one half cup

Method:

Heat the oven to 375. Drain the liquid off the lima beans and save it. Place the drained beans into an eight by eight-inch baking dish. Pour the bean liquid and the olive oil into a skillet and mix well, then mix in the thyme, lemon juice, dry mustard, cumin, salt, and pepper and heat until the mix is warm. Then pour this over the lima beans and cover with the nutritional yeast. Bake the casserole for thirty minutes.

Nutrition: Calories 194, 9 grams fiber, 7 grams fat, 6 grams protein, 19 grams carbs

8. SPROUT WRAPS

Prep fifteen min/serves two

Ingredients:

- Tortillas, whole wheat, two large
- Olive oil, one tablespoon
- Parsley, one-half cup chopped
- Lemon juice, one tablespoon
- Onion, green, two stalks
- Salt, one half teaspoon
- Black pepper, one teaspoon

- Bean sprouts, one cup
- Cucumber, one sliced thin

Method:

Place the tortilla wraps on a plate or work surface. Divide the bean sprouts, onion, cucumber, and parsley evenly between the two tortillas, placing the ingredients in the middle. Mix together the olive oil, pepper, salt, and lemon juice and pour this over the ingredients in the tortillas. Roll the tortillas and serve.

Nutrition: Calories 226, 8 grams fiber, 3 grams fat, 10 grams protein, 12 grams carbs

9. VEGETARIAN NACHOS

Prep fifteen minutes/serves six

Ingredients:

- Pita chips, whole wheat, three cups
- Nutritional yeast, one half cup
- Oregano, dried, one tablespoon minced
- Romaine lettuce, one cup chopped
- Grape tomatoes, one-half cup cut in quarters
- Olive oil, two tablespoons
- Lemon juice, one tablespoon
- Hummus, one-third cup prepared
- Black pepper, one half teaspoon
- Red onion, two tablespoons minced
- Tofu, one-half cup cut into small crumbles
- Black olives, two tablespoons chopped

Method:

Mix the hummus, pepper, olive oil, and lemon juice together in a mixing bowl. Spread a layer of the pita chips on a serving platter. Drizzle three-fourths of the hummus mix over the pita chips. Use the lettuce, red onion, tomatoes, and olives to garnish the hummus. Make a small mound of the leftover hummus in the middle of the chips, then garnish all with the oregano and the nutritional yeast.

Nutrition: Calories 159, 4 grams protein, 13 grams carbs, 2 grams fiber, 10 grams fat

10. VEGAN MACARONI AND CHEESE

Prep fifteen min/Cook twenty-five min/serves four

Ingredients:

- Elbow macaroni, whole grain, eight ounces, cooked
- Nutritional yeast, one quarter cup
- Garlic, minced, two tablespoons
- Apple cider vinegar, two teaspoons
- Broccoli, one head with florets cut into bite-sized pieces
- Water, one cup (more if needed)
- Garlic powder, one half teaspoon
- Avocado oil, two tablespoons
- Red pepper, flakes, one eighth teaspoon
- Onion, yellow, chopped, one cup
- Salt, one half teaspoon
- Russet potato, peeled and grated, one cup (about two small potatoes)
- Dry mustard powder, one half teaspoon
- Onion powder, one half teaspoon

Method:

Cook the broccoli for five minutes in boiling water. Add the cooked broccoli to the cooked pasta in a large mixing bowl. Cook the onion in the avocado oil for five minutes, then stir in the red pepper flakes, garlic, salt, mustard powder, garlic powder, grated potato, and onion powder. Cook this for three minutes and then pour in the water and mix well. Cook this for eight to ten minutes or until the potatoes are soft. Pour all of this mixture carefully into a blender and add in the nutritional yeast and the vinegar and then blend. When this is creamy and smooth, then pour it into the mixing bowl and mix well with the broccoli and pasta.

Nutrition: Calories 506, 9 grams fiber, 18 grams protein, 67 grams carbs, 22 grams fat

11. KALE, AVOCADO, AND BLACK BEAN BOWL

Prep twenty min/cook thirty min/serves four

Ingredients:

- Kale, one bunch with ribs removed and chopped into bite-sized pieces
- Brown rice, one cup rinsed and cooked
- Cherry tomatoes, cut in half, one half cup
- Salt, one quarter teaspoon
- Cayenne pepper, one quarter teaspoon
- Olive oil, two tablespoons
- Chili powder, one quarter teaspoon
- Jalapeno, one half, seeded and chopped finely
- Garlic, minced, two tablespoons
- Cumin, one half teaspoon
- Shallot, one chopped finely
- Avocado, one, peeled, pitted, cut into big chunks
- Black beans, two fifteen ounce cans drained and rinsed

- Salsa Verde, mild, one half cup

- Lime juice, one quarter cup

- Cilantro, chopped, one half cup

Method:

While the rice is being cooked, mix together the chopped kale, lime juice, jalapeno, olive oil, salt, and cumin and mix well. In a different bowl mix the avocado chunks with the salsa Verde, lime juice, and cilantro. Warm the beans in a pot over low heat, then stir in the cayenne pepper, chili powder, garlic, and shallot and cook for five minutes. Place the kale salad on four serving plates, dividing evenly. Divide the cooked bean mixture evenly among the four bowls and then top with the avocado salsa Verde mixture. Put the chopped cherry tomatoes on the top for a garnish.

Nutrition: Calories 424, 24 grams protein, 12 grams fiber, 57 grams carbs, 12 grams fat

12. PASTA ALA ERBE

Prep forty min/serves eight

Ingredients:

- Leafy greens, such as beet/chard/spinach, 1.5 pounds chop (no stems)

- Whole wheat fettuccine, one pound, cooked

- Olive oil, six tablespoons divide

- Tomato paste, two tablespoons

- Garlic, four cloves peeled and sliced thinly

- Hot water, one cup

- Salt, one half teaspoon

- Red pepper, crushed, one quarter teaspoon

- Rosemary, one teaspoon

Method:

Cook the garlic in four tablespoons of the olive oil for two minutes. Toss in the leafy greens a few at a time; as they cook down, they will begin to wilt, and soon, all will fit into the pan. Season with the rosemary, crushed pepper, and salt and stir well. Cook this mixture for ten minutes. Blend the water into the tomato paste. Add this to the skillet and let it simmer for fifteen minutes. Add in the cooked pasta to the skillet mix and toss well.

Nutrition info: Calories 355, 9 grams fiber, 48 grams carbs, 14 grams fat, 13 grams protein

13. ROAST BABY EGGPLANT

Prep twenty min/cook forty-five min/serves four

Ingredients:

To Cook

- Salt, one teaspoon
- Baby eggplant, eight
- Olive oil, two tablespoons
- Black pepper, one teaspoon

For Serving

- Nutritional yeast, one half cup
- Salt, one teaspoon
- Black pepper, one teaspoon
- Olive oil, two tablespoons

Method:

Heat the oven to 350. Wipe off the eggplants and then slice each one in half lengthwise. Lay the eggplant halves on a baking pan with the inside facing up and coat the insides with olive oil and then sprinkle on salt and pepper. Bake the baby eggplant for forty-five minutes or until they brown slightly and become soft. Just before you serve, the eggplants top each eggplant half with a teaspoon of the nutritional yeast and top that with the pepper, olive oil, and salt.

Nutrition per half an eggplant: Calories 44, 1 gram protein, 5 grams fiber, 1 gram carbs, 4 grams fat

14. COLLARD WRAPS

Prep twenty min/serves four

Ingredients:

Sauce

- Garlic powder, one teaspoon

- Black pepper, one teaspoon

- Cucumber, seeded and grated, one quarter cup

- White vinegar, one tablespoon

- Salt, one half teaspoon

- Olive oil, two tablespoons

- Dill, fresh, minced, two tablespoons

Wrap

- Green collard leaves, four large

- Cherry tomatoes, four cut in half

- Cucumber, one medium-sized cut in julienne strips

- Black olives, sliced, one quarter cup

- Red bell pepper, one half of one cut in julienne strips

- Purple onion, one-half cup diced fine

Method:

Place all of the ingredients for the sauce in a mixing bowl and mix well. Put the dressing in the refrigerator. Wash off the collard leaves and dry them thoroughly and then cut off the stem from each leaf. Cover each collard leaf with two tablespoons of the sauce you just made. In the middle of the collard leaf layer, all of the other ingredients. Fold the leaf up like a burrito by first folding the ends in and then rolling the leaf until it is all rolled. Cut each rolled leaf into slices and serve with more dressing for dipping.

Nutrition per wrap: Calories 165, 6 grams fiber, 7 grams carbs, 7 grams protein, 12 grams fat

SOUPS AND SALADS

1. GREEK STYLE SPRING SOUP

Prep ten minutes/cook twenty-five minutes/serves four to six

Ingredients:

- Chives, fresh minced for garnish
- Brown rice, one half cup
- Olive oil, two tablespoons
- Lemon juice, two tablespoons
- Vegetable broth, six cups
- Bay leaf, one
- Asparagus, one cup chop
- Salt, one half teaspoon
- Carrots, one cup diced
- Black pepper, one teaspoon
- Dill, fresh, chopped one half cup
- Turmeric, one teaspoon
- Onion, one small diced
- Rosemary, one teaspoon

Method:

Fry the onions for five minutes I the olive oil. Pour in one-half cup of the dill with the bay leaf and vegetable broth and boil. Mix in the rice and turn down the heat and let it simmer for fifteen minutes more. Put in the asparagus and the carrots and simmer ten more minutes.

Remove the bay leaf and then add the lemon juice and the remainder of the seasonings. Stir this well and serve, garnishing each of the servings with the remaining fresh dill.

Nutrition info: Calories 341, 30 grams carbs, 13 grams fiber, 3 grams fat, 12 grams protein

2. CILANTRO LIME COLESLAW

Prep ten min/serves five

Ingredients:

- Avocados, two
- Garlic, minced, one tablespoon
- Coleslaw, ready-made in bag, fourteen ounces
- Cilantro, fresh leaves, one-quarter cup minced
- Salt, one half teaspoon
- Lime juice, two tablespoons
- Water, one quarter cup

Method:

Except for the slaw mix, put all of the ingredients that are listed into a blender. Blend these ingredients well until they are creamy and smooth. Mix the coleslaw mix in with this dressing and then toss it gently to mix it well. Keep the mixed coleslaw in the refrigerator until you are ready to serve. It needs to chill for at least one hour.

Nutrition: Calories 119, 3 grams protein, 4 grams fiber, 3 grams carbs, 9 grams fat

3. PINEAPPLE AMBROSIA

Prep thirty min/cook fifteen min/serves four

Ingredients:

- Pineapple, fresh chopped, one cup
- Orange zest, two teaspoons
- Apples, fresh sliced, one cup
- Tofu, soft, pureed, one half cup
- Orange slices, one cup
- Strawberries, sliced, one cup
- Orange juice, three tablespoons
- Lemon juice, one third cup
- Cornstarch, one tablespoon
- Grapes, one cup
- Coconut, unsweetened shredded, one half cup

Method:

Use a large-sized mixing bowl to mix the fruits together and then put it in the refrigerator. In a small pot, mix together the lemon juice with the cornstarch and keep stirring until they are mixed well. Add in the orange juice and place the saucepan over medium-high heat. Cook the mix for five to ten minutes while the mixture gets thicker, stirring constantly. When the mixture is thick, then take the saucepan off of the heat and let it get cool completely. When the mixture has cooled completely, then blends in the orange zest and the pureed tofu. Allow this mix to rest in the refrigerator for one hour until it becomes chilled. Pour the dressing over the fruit before serving.

Nutrition: Calories 257, 44 grams carbs, 8 grams protein, 8 grams fat, 5 grams fiber

4. PASTA FAGIOLI

Prep ten min/cook one hour thirty min/serves eight

Ingredients:

- Olive oil, three tablespoons
- Whole wheat pasta, one pound any style, cook by package directions
- Basil, dried, one and one half teaspoons
- Onion, one, peeled and cut into small chunks
- Navy beans, one fifteen ounce can drain and rinse
- Garlic, minced, two tablespoons
- Cannellini beans, one fifteen ounce can drain and rinse
- Tomato sauce, one twenty-nine ounce can
- Salt, one half teaspoon
- Water, five and one half cups
- Parsley, one tablespoon
- Oregano, dried, one and one half teaspoons

Method:

In the olive oil fry the onion and garlic for five minutes in a large pot. Lower the heat and add the parsley, oregano, cannellini beans, basil, water, salt, navy beans, and tomato sauce, stir well and simmer for one hour. Mix in the cooked pasta and simmer five more minutes.

Nutrition info: Calories 403, 8 grams fat, 8 grams fiber, 68 grams carbs, 16 grams protein

Prep twenty min/cook one hour ten min/serves eight

Ingredients:

- Olive oil, one tablespoon
- Crushed tomatoes, one twenty-eight ounce can
- Cabbage, one head, remove core and chop
- Wild rice, one half cup uncooked
- Thyme, crushed, one half teaspoon
- Onion, one chopped
- Celery, three stalks sliced thin
- Water, three cups
- Carrots, three sliced thin
- Red beans, one fifteen ounce can with liquid
- Bay leaf, one
- Tomato sauce, one eight-ounce can
- Salt, one half teaspoon

Method:

Cook the onion in hot olive oil in a large skillet for five minutes. Stir in the water. Add in the crushed tomatoes, beans, tomato sauce, carrots, rice, celery, and cabbage and mix this together well. Mix in salt, bay leaf, and thyme. Boil the soup for one minute, and then lower the heat, simmering for one hour. Remove the bay leaf and serve.

Nutrition info: Calories 404, 37 grams carbs, 10 grams fiber, 21 grams fat, 21 grams protein

Prep thirty min/serves fifteen

Ingredients:

- Lemon juice, two tablespoons
- Green grapes, two cups
- Red grapes, two cups
- Orange juice, one quarter cup
- Apples, two, cored and cubed
- Strawberries, halved, two cups
- Bananas, three sliced
- Cantaloupe, cubed, two cups
- Watermelon, seedless, cubed, four cups
- Honeydew, cubed, two cups

Method:

In a small bowl, blend well the orange juice and the lemon juice. In a very large-sized mixing bowl, mix together all of the fruits and immediately cover with the juice mix. Toss the juice mix with the fruit to ensure that all of the pieces are coated. Refrigerate for one hour and serve.

Nutrition: Calories 185, 7 grams fat, 48 grams carbs, 8 grams fiber, 5 grams protein

7. VEGAN COBB SALAD

Prep twenty min/serves four

Ingredients:

Salad

- Greens – chopped romaine, spring mix, or baby spinach or a mix of these, twelve cups
- Avocados, two sliced
- Chickpeas, two fifteen ounce cans drained and rinsed
- Tempeh (soybean) bacon
- Red onion, chopped, one half cup
- Grape tomatoes, cut in half, one cup
- Cucumber, one large peeled and chopped
- Corn, thawed frozen or fresh, one half cup
- Carrots, grated, one cup

Vinaigrette

- Salt, one half teaspoon
- Balsamic vinegar, one third cup
- Olive oil, one half cup
- Dijon mustard, one tablespoon
- Garlic, minced, one teaspoon
- Black pepper, one half teaspoon

Method:

Mix together well in a small bowl or a glass jar all of the ingredients for the vinaigrette dressing and put it in the refrigerator until you are ready to serve the salad. Follow the directions on the wrapper to cook the tempeh bacon. Divide the greens between four bowls or salad plates. Arrange on the top of the greens equal amounts of the red onion, tempeh bacon, tomatoes, carrots, corn, cucumber, and chickpeas. Lay the slices of avocado over the ingredients on top of the lettuce and drizzle on the amount of the salad dressing you prefer.

Nutrition: Calories 385, 54 grams carbs, 20 grams fiber, 11 grams fat, 19 grams protein

8. TOMATO SALAD

Prep fifteen min/serves six

Ingredients:

- Olive oil, one quarter cup
- Grape tomatoes, one pint halved
- Basil leaves, chopped fresh, one quarter cup
- Balsamic vinegar, two tablespoons
- Yellow tomatoes, sliced thin, one cup
- Salt, one half teaspoon
- Red tomatoes, sliced thin, one cup
- Black pepper, one teaspoon
- Chives, two tablespoons chop fine

Method:

Mix together in a medium-sized bowl the balsamic vinegar, salt, pepper, and olive oil until they are well blended. Put the tomatoes into this mix and toss them gently to coat them well. Sprinkle the top of the mix with the fresh basil and the chives.

Nutrition: Calories 105, 1 gram protein, 10 grams fat, 9 grams fiber, 6 grams carbs

9. SWEET POTATO CAULIFLOWER SALAD

Prep twenty min/cook thirty min/serves eight

Ingredients:

- Sweet potatoes, one and one-half pound, cut into one half inch wide wedges
- Salt, one teaspoon
- Cranberries, dried, one half cup
- Cauliflower, one small head broken into florets
- Lettuce, any variety, torn, eight cups
- Balsamic vinegar, three tablespoons
- Olive oil, seven tablespoons divided
- Black pepper, one teaspoon

Method:

Heat the oven to 425. Mix together in a medium-sized bowl the cauliflower florets and the sweet potato wedges with the salt, pepper, and three tablespoons of the olive oil. Spread these out on a baking sheet and bake them for thirty minutes and then let them cool down slightly. During the time that the veggies are roasting mix together in a mixing bowl, the balsamic vinegar and the remainder of the olive oil. Then add in the lettuce, dried cranberries, and the cooled roasted veggies. Toss this mixture well to coat all pieces and serve immediately.

Nutrition: Calories 150, 5 grams protein, 3 grams fiber, 12 grams fat, 11 grams carbs

10. TROPICAL STYLE RADICCHIO SALAD

Prep fifteen min/serves six

Ingredients:

- Radicchio, two medium heads cut into quarters from top to the bottom
- Black pepper, one half teaspoon
- Coconut oil, two tablespoons

- Pineapple, fresh, fine chop, two cups
- Salt, one half teaspoon
- Basil leaves, chopped, one-quarter cup firmly packed
- Orange juice, two tablespoons

Method:

Heat the oven to 450. Brush the coconut oil on both sides of the pieces of radicchio. Bake the radicchio for ten minutes, turning them over after five minutes. Allow the radicchio to slightly cool. When it has cooled to room temperature, slice it very thinly, to look like chopped cabbage, and then place it in a large-sized bowl. Add in the basil, pepper, orange juice, salt, and pineapple and toss the ingredients gently but well enough to mix them together and coat all the pieces well. You can serve it right away or keep it in the refrigerator for no more than one day.

Nutrition: Calories 40, 2 grams fat, 1 gram fiber, 5 grams carbs, 3 grams protein

11. MEXICAN STYLE VEGETABLE SOUP

Prep fifteen min/cook thirty-five min/serves six

Ingredients:

- Diced tomatoes with green chilies, canned, one fourteen to fifteen ounce can
- Yellow onion, one, peeled and diced
- Cilantro, chopped, one half cup
- Carrots, two peeled and diced
- Lime juice, two tablespoons
- Olive oil, two tablespoons
- Corn, frozen or canned, two cups
- Garlic, minced, two tablespoons

128

- Salt, one teaspoon

- Vegetable broth, five cups

- Black pepper, one teaspoon

- Cumin, ground, one teaspoon

- Zucchini, one medium chopped into bite-sized chunks

- Oregano, dried, one teaspoon

- Green beans, frozen or canned, one cup

- Red bell pepper, one diced

Method:

Fry the onion and carrots for three minutes in the olive oil. Stir in the garlic and cook for two more minutes. Mix in the pepper, salt, tomatoes, zucchini, vegetables broth, bell pepper, green beans, cumin, and oregano. Mix all these together well and bring the mix to a full boil. Simmer the soup over a lower heat for twenty to twenty-five minutes until all of the vegetables are soft. Mix in the lime juice, cilantro, and corn and cook for five more minutes and serve.

Nutrition: Calories 103, 3 grams protein, 4 grams fiber, 3 grams fat, 18 grams carbs

12. TROPICAL FRUIT SALAD

Prep ten minutes/serves two

Ingredients:

- Dragon fruit, one half of one

- Mango, one half of one

- Lime juice, one tablespoon

- Strawberries, twelve

- Kiwi, two

Method:

Peel all of the fruits and then chop them into small, bite-sized pieces. Dump all of the chunks of fruit into a large-sized mixing bowl. Drizzle the lime juice over the fruit and toss the fruit gently to coat all of the pieces with the juice. Serve immediately

Nutrition: Calories 154, 38 grams carbs, 5 grams fiber, 1 gram fat, 3 grams protein

13. CHERRY BERRY SALAD

Prep ten min/serves six

Ingredients:

- Blackberries, one cup
- Strawberries, cleaned, two cups quartered
- Lemon juice, three tablespoons
- Cherries, seeded, cut in half, one cup
- Cardamom, one quarter teaspoon
- Raspberries, one cup
- Cinnamon, one half teaspoon
- Blueberries, one cup
- Mint, fresh, three tablespoons

Method:

In a small-sized mixing bowl, mix the lemon juice and the spices together well. In a medium-sized bowl, mix the fruits together with the lemon juice and mint mixture. Toss the fruits gently but thoroughly to coat all of the pieces. This will keep fresh in the refrigerator for two to three days.

Nutrition: Calories 113, 1 gram protein, 1 gram fat, 27 grams carbs, 6 grams fiber

14. WINTER VEGETABLE SALAD

Prep ten min/cook forty min/serves three

Ingredients:

Roasted Vegetables

- Red onion, one
- Olive oil, one tablespoon
- Butternut squash, one small
- Salt, one half teaspoon
- Baby red potatoes, ten
- Black pepper, one teaspoon
- Carrots, two
- Parsnips, two

Salad

- Salt, one half teaspoon
- Salad mixed greens, four cups packed
- Rosemary, one teaspoon
- Black pepper, one teaspoon
- Coriander, dried, one tablespoon
- Balsamic vinegar, two tablespoons
- Parsley, fresh, two tablespoons chop fine
- Olive oil, one tablespoon
- Marjoram, one teaspoon
- Basil, dried, two tablespoons

Method:

Heat the oven to 400. Wash the carrots, potatoes, and parsnips and dry them with a paper towel. Wipe off the squash and the onion and peel them. Chop all of the vegetables into bite-sized chunks. Place all of the chunks of veggies into a large-sized bowl with the salt, pepper, and olive oil. Toss all of the vegetables in the bowl with the olive oil until they are coated well. Spread out the oiled veggies on a baking sheet and bake them in the oven for forty minutes. While the veggies are roasting, you can mix up the dressing for the salad. Mix the balsamic vinegar with the olive oil and all of the salt, pepper, and herbs. When you take the vegetables from the oven, divide them into three servings and pour the dressing over the top of the veggie servings as personally desired.

Nutrition: Calories 483, 85 grams carbs, 17 grams fiber, 12 grams fat, 11 grams protein

15. HOMEMADE VEGETABLE BROTH

Prep ten min/cook one hour/makes ten one-cup servings

Keeps in the refrigerator for five days or freezer for one month

Ingredients:

- Salt, one teaspoon

- Water, ten cups

- Black pepper, two teaspoons

- Tomato paste, five tablespoons

- Oil, one tablespoon of olive, avocado, or coconut

- Greens (collard, kale, spinach), one cup chopped

- Celery, four stalks chopped fine

- Parsley, fresh or dried, one quarter cup

- Carrots, four chopped fine leave skin on

- Thyme, dried, one tablespoon

- Garlic, four cloves cut in half

- Rosemary, dried, two tablespoons

- Onion, one medium peeled and chopped

Method:

In a large pot fry the carrots, garlic, celery, and onion for five minutes over medium-high heat in the oil of choice. Blend in the remaining of the listed ingredients and bring the whole mix to a boil. Let the soup simmer over a low heat for one hour. Once this is finished cooking, let it cool for thirty minutes and then strain out the veggies and store the broth in the freezer or the refrigerator. The veggies can be pureed and kept in small amounts in the freezer (think plastic ice cube tray). These can be used to flavor other soups.

Nutrition per one cup: Calories 42, 6 grams carbs, 2 grams fiber, 2 grams fat, 3 grams protein

DRESSINGS AND SAUCES

For any of these recipes, just put all of the ingredients into a shaker jar or a blender and mix them together well.

1. LEMON POPPY SEED

Prep five min/makes one cup

Ingredients:

- Dijon mustard, one tablespoon
- Olive oil, one half cup
- Maple syrup, one tablespoon
- Lemon juice, three tablespoons
- Poppy seeds, one tablespoon

2. MAPLE MUSTARD DRESSING

Prep five min/makes one cup

Ingredients:

- Dijon mustard, two tablespoons
- Olive oil, one quarter cup
- Garlic powder, one quarter teaspoon
- Maple syrup, two tablespoons
- Lemon juice, one tablespoon

3. GREEK DRESSING

Prep five min/makes one cup

Ingredients:

- Oregano, dried, one and one half teaspoon
- Olive oil, one quarter cup
- Black pepper, one quarter teaspoon
- Lemon juice, one quarter cup
- Salt, one quarter teaspoon
- Dijon mustard, one tablespoon
- Garlic powder, one quarter teaspoon

4. MISO DRESSING

Prep five min/makes one cup

Ingredients:

- Rice vinegar, one half cup
- Sesame oil, one teaspoon
- Peanut oil, one quarter cup
- Ginger, ground, one tablespoon
- Agave nectar, two tablespoons
- Miso paste, white, one tablespoon

5. CHERRY TOMATO DRESSING

Prep five min/Makes one cup

Ingredients:

- Cherry tomatoes
- Paprika, one half teaspoon
- Black pepper, one quarter teaspoon
- Balsamic vinegar, one quarter cup
- Salt, one quarter teaspoon
- Olive oil, one quarter cup
- Garlic powder, one quarter teaspoon
- Agave nectar, one tablespoon
- Onion powder, one half teaspoon

6. SWEET DILL DRESSING

Prep five minutes/makes one cup

Ingredients:

- Nutritional yeast, one quarter cup
- Water, three tablespoons
- Vegenaise, three tablespoons
- Garlic powder, one quarter teaspoon
- Dill, dried, one teaspoon
- Agave nectar, one tablespoon
- Apple cider vinegar, one tablespoon

7. CHIPOTLE LIME DRESSING

Prep five min/makes one cup

Ingredients:

- Vegenaise, three tablespoons
- Garlic powder, one quarter teaspoon
- Lime juice, three tablespoons
- Paprika, one quarter teaspoon
- Red pepper, one chopped
- Agave nectar, one tablespoon

8. BALSAMIC VINAIGRETTE

Prep five min/makes one cup

Ingredients:

- Olive oil, one half cup
- Black pepper, one quarter teaspoon
- Agave nectar, one tablespoon
- Balsamic vinegar, one quarter cup
- Salt, one quarter teaspoon
- Dijon mustard, one tablespoon
- Garlic powder, one quarter teaspoon

9. APPLESAUCE SALAD DRESSING

Prep ten min/makes one cup

Ingredients:

- Chickpea miso, one teaspoon
- Applesauce, unsweetened, one quarter cup
- Black pepper, one eighth teaspoon
- Salt, one quarter teaspoon
- Cinnamon, one teaspoon
- Apple cider vinegar, two tablespoons
- Cumin, one quarter teaspoon
- Balsamic vinegar, one tablespoon
- Dijon mustard, one teaspoon

10. CURRIED ALMOND DRESSING

Prep fifteen min/makes one cup

Ingredients:

- Garlic, minced, one tablespoon
- Almonds, raw, one half cup
- Curry powder, one eighth teaspoon
- Apple cider vinegar, two tablespoons
- Black pepper, one eighth teaspoon
- Agave nectar, two tablespoons
- Salt, one half teaspoon
- Water, two-thirds cup

- Dijon mustard, one half teaspoon
- Ginger, ground, one teaspoon

11. TAHINI CITRUS DRESSING

Prep fifteen min/makes one half cup

Ingredients:

- Orange juice, three tablespoons
- Black pepper, one half teaspoon
- Lemon juice, one tablespoon
- Salt, one half teaspoon
- Tahini, two tablespoons
- Garlic, minced, one tablespoon
- Apple cider vinegar, one tablespoon
- Ginger, ground, one teaspoon
- Agave nectar, two tablespoons
- Dijon mustard, two teaspoons

12. MOROCCAN CARROT DIP

Prep fifteen min/makes one cup

Ingredients:

- Carrot, raw, one cup cut into small chunks
- Water, one half cup
- Cashews, raw, one third cup
- Black pepper, one quarter teaspoon

- Apple cider vinegar, two teaspoons
- Salt, one half teaspoon
- Garlic, minced, one tablespoon
- Fennel, one quarter teaspoon
- Ginger, ground, one teaspoon
- Coriander, ground, one half teaspoon
- Cinnamon, one teaspoon
- Cumin, ground, one half teaspoon

13. WALNUT BASIL DRESSING

Prep ten minutes/makes twelve servings

Ingredients:

- Lemon juice, three tablespoons
- Basil leaves, one cup packed loosely, chopped fine
- Water, two to four tablespoons as needed
- Walnuts, one-half cup crushed
- Salt, one quarter teaspoon
- Olive oil, one quarter cup
- Garlic, minced, one tablespoon
- Nutritional yeast, one quarter cup

14. COLESLAW DRESSING

Prep five min/makes twelve servings

Ingredients:

- Dijon mustard, one tablespoon
- Vegenaise, one half cup
- Celery seed, one teaspoon
- Apple cider vinegar, two tablespoons
- Onion powder, one teaspoon
- Agave nectar, one tablespoon

15. CATALINA DRESSING

Prep five min/makes twelve servings

Ingredients:

- Tomato sauce, one quarter cup
- Dry mustard, one half teaspoon
- Olive oil, one quarter cup
- Chili powder, one half teaspoon
- Apple cider vinegar, three tablespoons
- Onion powder, one half teaspoon

DAILY SNACKS

Here are some suggestions for daily snacks that will keep you energized and still stay vegan.

- Frozen red or green grapes
- Celery sticks stuffed with nut butter and dotted with raisins
- Spiced nuts
- Baked veggie chips
- Sliced bananas spread with peanut butter
- Bean dip and pita chips
- Granola
- Popcorn
- Salsa and tortilla chips
- Oatmeal with seeds, nuts, or fruit
- Veggie or fruit smoothies
- Hummus with veggie sticks or pita chips
- Rice cakes spread with mashed avocado
- Fruit jerky
- Roasted chickpeas
- Edamame (soybeans)
- Trail mix
- Guacamole with veggie sticks or pita chips

1. BASIL BERRY LEMONADE SORBET

Prep five min/chill twenty min/serves six

Ingredients:
Lemon juice, four tablespoons
Mixed berries, frozen, six cups
Basil, fresh, one cup lightly packed
Vegan sugar, one cup
Water, one cup

Method:

Blend the water and sugar in a pot and heat it on medium-high until the sugar is dissolved, stirring often. Add in the basil and remove the pot from the heat and let it sit for fifteen minutes. Strain the syrup into a bowl and throw away the basil. Put the bowl in the refrigerator until the liquid is cold. When it has completely chilled put the liquid in a blender with the lemon juice and berries and blend until all ingredients are smooth. Pour it into an eight-inch square baking pan, preferably a metal one, and cover the dish with plastic wrap. Set it in the freezer until the liquid is firm which takes about two hours.

Nutrition: Calories 195, 4 grams fiber, 1 grams fat, 53 grams carbs, 1 gram protein

2. LEMON TARTS

Prep twenty min/chill two hours/serves three

Ingredients:
CRUST
Lemon zest, one teaspoon
Lemon juice, two tablespoons
Maple syrup, two tablespoons
Coconut oil, two tablespoons melted
Cashews, raw, three-fourths cup

Coconut, shredded, one cup

FILLING
Salt, one fourth teaspoon
Vanilla extract, one teaspoon
Lemon zest, one tablespoon
Maple syrup, one fourth cup
Coconut milk, canned, one fourth cup
Coconut oil, one third cup
Lemon juice, one half cup
Cashews, raw, one cup, soak in water for four hours

Method:

Lightly oil three tart dishes, or one nine-inch tart pan, using coconut oil. Make the crust by mixing the cashews and shredded coconut and crush the cashews to make small bits. Blend in the lemon juice, lemon zest, maple syrup, and coconut oil until you have a paste. Press this paste into the tart pan(s). Then blend together all of the ingredients to make the filling until the mix is creamy and smooth. Pour the mix into the tart pan(s) and chill for two hours.

Nutrition: Calories 357, 7 grams protein, 3 grams fiber, 29 grams carbs, 25 grams fat

3. CHOCOLATE PUDDING
Prep two min/cook five min/serves six

Ingredients:
Salt, one eighth teaspoon
Vanilla extract, two teaspoons
Maple syrup, six tablespoons
Cacao powder, raw, one half cup
Coconut cream, canned, one and one half cups

Method:

Cream together in a pot over low heat the maple syrup, cacao, and maple syrup until all ingredients are smooth. Cook this mix for three minutes. Mix in the vanilla and salt and remove the pot from the heat. Pour it into a bowl and let it chill before serving.

Nutrition: Calories 272, 3 grams protein, 3 grams fiber, 21 grams carbs, 21 grams fat

4. ONE MINUTE BROWNIE

Prep two min/cook one min/serves one

Ingredients:
Maple syrup, one tablespoon
Dark chocolate chunks, one tablespoon
Almond milk, one quarter cup
Coconut flour, one tablespoon
Cocoa powder, one tablespoon
Baking powder, one half teaspoon

Method:

Use some spray oil to oil a microwave-safe small bowl. Mix all of the ingredients together and microwave for one minute and stir well.

Nutrition: Calories 129, 2 grams fiber, 4 grams fat, 3 grams protein, 3 grams carbs

5. PEANUT BUTTER FUDGE

Prep thirty min/makes twenty pieces

Ingredients:
Vanilla extract, one teaspoon
Maple syrup, three tablespoons
Coconut oil, melted, one half cup
Creamy peanut butter, one cup
Coconut flakes, unsweetened, two cups

Method:

Use spray oil on an eight-inch square pan. Cream the shredded coconut in a food processor until it forms a buttery substance. Put the coconut butter into a bowl and blend in the coconut oil and peanut butter. Then add in the vanilla and mix once more. Spoon the mix into the pan and let it set.

146

Nutrition: Calories 164, 4 grams protein, 2 grams fiber, 5 grams carbs, 16 grams fat

6. APPLE CAKE

Prep twenty min/cook sixty min/yield twelve slices

Ingredients:

Sesame seeds, three tablespoons
Applesauce, one half cup
Vegan brown sugar, light, one cup plus two tablespoons
Cinnamon, ground, two teaspoons
Olive oil, one cup
Raisins, one half cup
Walnuts, chopped, one half cup
Almond milk, one cup
Apples, four, peel halve core and slice thin
Vanilla, one teaspoon
Wheat flour, two and one half cups
Baking powder, two teaspoons

Method:

Heat the oven to 375. Cream together the applesauce, sugar, and olive oil in a large bowl. Then blend in the baking powder, almond milk, wheat flour, and vanilla and stir until well mixed. Use spray oil to oil a nine-inch square baking dish. Mix together the apples, walnuts, raisins, brown sugar, and the cinnamon. Put half of the batter for the cake into the baking dish and then top with the apple mixture. Then pour the rest of the batter for the cake on top. Bake the cake for fifty minutes.

Nutrition: Calories 345, 5 grams fiber, 22 grams fat, 3 grams protein, 35 grams carbs

7. BANANA PEANUT BUTTER YOGURT BOWL

Prep five min/serves four

Ingredients:

Nutmeg, one teaspoon
Flax seed meal, one quarter cup
Creamy peanut butter, all-natural, one quarter cup

Bananas, two medium-sized sliced
Soy yogurt, vanilla flavor, four cups

Method:

Divide the yogurt among four bowls and top with the slices of bananas. Soften the butter in the microwave for forty seconds and then put one tablespoon into each bowl, then garnish with the nutmeg and flax seed meal.

Nutrition: Calories 292, 15 grams fat, 24 grams carbs, 29 grams protein, 3 grams fiber

8. VANILLA MAPLE BAKED PEARS
Prep five min/cook twenty-five min/serves four

Ingredients:
Vanilla, one teaspoon
Cinnamon, ground, one quarter teaspoon
Maple syrup, one half cup
Anjou pears, four

Method:

Heat the oven to 375. Use spray oil to oil a baking sheet. Cut the four pears in half lengthwise. Slice off a tiny sliver of the outside of the pear so that it will sit still on the baking sheet. Sprinkle ground cinnamon on all of the pear halves. Blend together the maple syrup and the vanilla. Drizzle this over the pears and bake for twenty minutes.

9. MAPLE STRAWBERRY YOGURT
Prep ten min/serves four

Ingredients:
Strawberries, fresh, one pint
Almonds, toasted and sliced, four tablespoons
Maple syrup, four teaspoons
Soy yogurt, plain, three cups

10. RASPBERRY GELATO
Prep thirty min/set twelve hours

Ingredients:
Raspberries, fresh, two pounds, cleaned and cut in quarters
Lemon juice, two tablespoons
Vegan sugar, granulated, one cup
Cornstarch, two tablespoons
Soy yogurt, three cups

Method:

Blend all of the ingredients except the raspberries in a pot over low heat until it boils. Let the mix cool for ten minutes while you puree the raspberries. Blend the raspberries into the mix and stir together well. Freeze the mix for ten hours and serve.

ENERGIZING AND HEALTHY DRINKS

1. GINGERBREAD MAPLE LATTE
Prep five min/cook ten min/serves two

Ingredients:
Almond milk, one and one half cup
Maple syrup, one tablespoon
Ginger, ground, one fourth teaspoon
Cinnamon, ground, one fourth teaspoon
Nutmeg, ground, one fourth teaspoon
Prepared coffee, one half cup

Put ingredients into a small pot over medium heat and warm for five minutes, stirring often. Pour into two mugs and add whipped coconut cream if you wish.

2. HOT APPLE CIDER
Prep fifteen min/cook twenty min/serves four

Ingredients:
Orange, one half sliced
Lemon juice, one teaspoon
Ginger, ground, one teaspoon
Cardamom, ground, one teaspoon
Cloves, ground, one teaspoon
Apple juice, four cups
Cinnamon sticks, four

Put ingredients into a small pot over medium heat and warm until almost boiling. Pour into four cups and drop in a cinnamon stick.

3. CHAI TEA

Prep five min/steep thirty min

Ingredients:
Maple syrup, one tablespoon
Cashew milk, one cup
Black peppercorns, one tablespoon
Ginger, ground, one tablespoon
Cloves, ground, one tablespoon
Cardamom, ground, one tablespoon
Cinnamon, ground, one tablespoon
Black tea, eight bags
Water, five cups

Place the spices in a pot over medium heat with the tea bags and the water. Boil it and then let it simmer for twenty minutes. Take out the tea bags and let it simmer for another twenty minutes. Strain the tea and serve.

4. MULLED CIDER

Prep ten min

Ingredients:
Orange, two sliced thinly
Cloves, whole, one tablespoon
Allspice, one teaspoon
Cinnamon sticks, four
Maple syrup, four tablespoons
Apple cider, eight cups
Cranberry juice, not cocktail, eight cups

Blend the apple cider and the cranberry juice in a pot over medium heat and stir in the maple syrup. Add in everything else except the orange slices and boil. Then let it simmer for ten minutes. Strain the mix well and serve with slices of orange.

5. PEPPERMINT HOT COCOA
Prep three min/cook ten min/serves four

Ingredients:
Peppermint sticks, four, crushed for garnish
Coconut cream, whipped, for garnish
Peppermint extract, one quarter teaspoon
Maple syrup, two tablespoons
Dark chocolate bar, non-dairy, four ounces
Almond milk, two cups

Warm the milk for five minutes and then add in the maple syrup and the chocolate and simmer while the chocolate melts, stirring often. Blend in the peppermint extract and remove from the heat. Pour into mugs and top with whipped coconut cream and crushed peppermint stick.

6. METABOLISM BOOSTER
Prep ten min/serves one

Ingredients:
Water, 3 cups
Lemon, one, sliced
Cucumber, one, sliced
Mint, two leaves
Ice

Special water for a quicker metabolism! With the lemon acting as an energizer, cucumber for a refreshing taste, and mint to help your stomach digest, this water is perfect!
All you will have to do is get out a pitcher, place all of the ingredients in, and allow the ingredients to soak overnight for maximum benefits.

MEASUREMENTS CONVERSION CHART

Liquid (Fluid or Volume) Measurements (approximate):

1 teaspoon equals		1/3 tablespoon	5 ml
1 tablespoon	1/2 fluid ounce	3 teaspoons	15 ml
2 tablespoons	1 fluid ounce	1/8 cup, 6 teaspoons	30 ml
1/4 cup	2 fluid ounces	4 tablespoons	59 ml
1/3 cup	2 2/3 fluid ounces	5 tablespoons + 1 teaspoon	79 ml
1/2 cup	4 fluid ounces	8 tablespoons	118 ml
2/3 cup	5 1/3 fluid ounces	10 tablespoons + 2 teaspoons	158 ml
3/4 cup	6 fluid ounces	12 tablespoons	177 ml
7/8 cup	7 fluid ounces	14 tablespoons	207 ml
1 cup	8 fluid ounces / 1/2 pint	16 tablespoons	237 ml
2 cups	16 fluid ounces / 1 pint	32 tablespoons	473 ml
4 cups	32 fluid ounces	1 quart	946 ml
1 pint	16 fluid ounces/ 1 pint	32 tablespoons	473 ml
2 pints	32 fluid ounces	1 quart	946 ml, 0.946 liters
8 pints	1 gallon/ 128 fluid ounces		3785 ml, 3.78 liters
4 quarts	1 gallon/ 128 fluid ounces		3785 ml, 3.78 liters
1 liter	1.057 quarts		1000 ml
1 gallon	128 fluid ounces		3785 ml, 3.78 liters

Dry (Weight) label appears at the left of the table, between "1/2 cup" and "2/3 cup" rows.

Measurements (approximate):

1 ounce		30 grams (28.35 g)
2 ounces		55 grams
3 ounces		85 grams

4 ounces	1/4 pound	125 grams
8 ounces	1/2 pound	240 grams
12 ounces	3/4 pound	375 grams
16 ounces	1 pound	454 grams
32 ounces	2 pounds	907 grams

CHAPTER 4: TWO WEEK MEAL PLAN

This is a suggestion of meals for the first two weeks of your beginning into your vegan diet to support your athletic lifestyle. All of the recipes can be found in this book.

WEEK ONE

Monday

Breakfast: Vegan Tacos

Lunch: Cucumber Tomato Toast

Dinner: Mushroom Risotto with Cauliflower Rice

Tuesday

Breakfast: Breakfast Millet with Apples

Lunch: Orange Banana Smoothie

Dinner: Roasted Pepper Pasta Salad

Wednesday

Breakfast: Quinoa Oatmeal

Lunch: Tofu Scramble with Spinach

Dinner: Mini Pitas with Black Beans

Thursday

Breakfast: Hemp Porridge with Pears and Blueberries

Lunch: Cauliflower Fried Rice

Dinner: White Bean Bolognese

Friday

Breakfast:	Vegan Omelet with Mushrooms
Lunch:	Potato Salad with Mustard Sauce
Dinner:	Lentils with Cauliflower and Sweet Potatoes

Saturday

Breakfast:	Papaya Mango with Baby Spinach and Peanut Butter Sauce
Lunch:	Vegan Pinto Beans
Dinner:	Zucchini Lasagna

Sunday

Breakfast:	Banana French Toast
Lunch:	Grilled Eggplant Rolls
Dinner:	Veggie Rice Skillet

Monday

Breakfast: Chickpea Toast

Lunch: Sweet Potato Squash Patties

Dinner: Korean Pseudo Beef Bowl

Tuesday

Breakfast: Lentil and Broccoli cutlets

Lunch: Sprout Wraps

Dinner: Mediterranean Spaghetti Squash

Wednesday

Breakfast: Tofu Scramble with Onions and Peppers

Lunch: Macaroni and Cheese

Dinner: Veggies and Farro

Thursday

Breakfast: Maple Oatmeal

Lunch: Pasta ala Erbe

Dinner: Eggplant Casserole

Friday

Breakfast: Potato Hash with Mushrooms and Asparagus

Lunch: Corn and Okra Casserole

Dinner: Mushroom and Brown Rice Risotto

Saturday

Breakfast: Matcha Smoothie Bowl

Lunch: Stuffed Artichokes

Dinner: Creamy Curry Noodles

Sunday

Breakfast: Scrambled Tofu

Lunch: Lima Bean Casserole

Dinner: Roasted Vegetables

CONCLUSION

Thank you for making it through to the end of *The Vegan Fitness Cookbook*, let's hope it was informative and able to provide you with all of the tools you need to achieve your goals whatever they may be.

The next step is to begin to plan how the vegan way of eating will fit into your particular way of life. Only you will know the goals that you have for your particular level of athletic activity. Is your goal to lose weight and become lean? Is your goal to build muscle and compete in bodybuilding or weightlifting competitions? Is your goal to become an endurance athlete who competes in marathons? Whatever your personal goal is, you will be able to build a vegan meal plan that is based on your personal needs. And you have all that you need in this book to get you started.

Finally, if you found this book useful in any way, a review on Amazon is always appreciated!